ED YOUNG

LIFE'S TOO SHORT

DOING WHAT IT TAKES TO MAKE OUR LIVES COUNT

LIFE'S TOO SHORT

(ey) STUDY GUIDE

Copyright © 2008 by Edwin B. Young. All rights reserved.

Written permission must be secured from the author to use or reproduce any part of this book, except for occasional page copying for personal study or brief quotations in critical reviews or articles.

Ed Young Resources
Published in Dallas, TX by Creality Publishing.

All Scripture quotations, unless otherwise noted, are taken from The Holy Bible, New International Version (North American Edition), copyright © 1973, 1978, 1984 by the International Bible Society. Used by permission of Zondervan Publishing House.

Any emphases or parenthetical comments within Scripture are the author's own.

ISBN 13: 978-1-934146-81-1

Design and Layout: Jason Acker Design

CONTENTS

Week 1	...Not To Fish	7
	Devotionals	16
Week 2	...To Be Negative	27
	Devotionals	38
Week 3	...To Be Envious	49
	Devotionals	60
Week 4	...To Be Selfish	71
	Devotionals	82
Week 5	...To Lie	93
	Devotionals	104

LEADER'S GUIDE

Week 1	...Not To Fish	115
Week 2	...To Be Negative	119
Week 3	...To Be Envious	123
Week 4	...To Be Selfish	127
Week 5	...To Lie	131

HOW TO USE THIS BOOK

Small Groups are a vital part of how we do ministry at Fellowship Church, just as they are in many churches around the world. There are a number of different theories on how small groups should work and they are all great in different ways. The book you are holding is written with our model in mind. So take a minute to read the following explanation, then feel free to adapt as necessary.

Each of our small groups practices a three part agenda in every meeting. That agenda includes a social time, a discussion time, and a prayer time. Each of these elements share equal importance, but not necessarily equal time. To help you get the most out of this book we have included an explanation of each of the parts.

The first element of every small group meeting should be a time of socializing. This phase of the meeting should be about 30% of your time together. Welcome everyone as they arrive at the host home, and make visitors feel welcome by introducing yourself and the other members of your small group. Enjoy some snacks, or if your group prefers, a meal together.

Then move on with second part of the meeting, the lesson. The lesson itself may take as much as 50% of your group's meeting time, but remember, it is not the most important element. You may want to start this phase of your meeting with a short "icebreaker" to get everyone talking. The questions in the "Start it Up" section of each chapter are what we refer to as "level the playing field" questions that everyone should be able to participate in, regardless of their level of spiritual maturity or Bible knowledge. As your group moves through the "Talk it Up" section in each chapter, remember that it is more important to finish on time than to finish each and every question. It is okay to skip some questions to be sure you allow enough time to take care of the third phase of the small group time: "Lift it Up."

The "Lift it Up" section is a vital part of every small group meeting and should be about 20% of the meeting. During this time you will be able to share with the group what God is doing in your life as well as asking the group to support you in specific prayers. To help focus this time, there are one or two questions at the end of each study that will prompt prayers based on the material you have just talked about. There is also a space for you to write down your prayer request(s) so you don't forget them and so you can communicate them clearly when it is your turn. Below that is a place to write down the prayer requests of the people in your group so you can remember and pray for each request throughout the week.

As an additional tool to assist you in your journey of spiritual development, there is a "Step it Up" section at the end of each session. This section consists of five devotional thoughts that reinforce the lesson you've just completed and are designed to help you develop a regular quiet time with God. To get the absolute most from this study, I challenge you to take five or ten minutes a day to read and apply these devotionals to your life. If your group meets twice a month or bi-weekly, choose five of the intervening days to incorporate these thoughts into your devotional life.

In select studies, we have incorporated special notes for youth groups using this material. You will notice a special icon (Y) used several times in each session. This indicates that there is a comment or question especially for youth included in the leader's guide for that part of the study. When you see that icon, simply turn to the leader's guide for that session in the back of the book and find the corresponding (Y) and letter (for instance, (Y)-a). These notes are designed to help each discussion time connect with the unique needs and issues of youth.

LIFE'S TOO SHORT

If you were given the opportunity to know exactly when you were going to die, would you want to know? And if you knew, would it change the way you live? Or would you go through life exactly the same—doing the same things, the same way for the same reasons? It's an interesting thought.

Mortality, though, isn't something we really like to consider. No one wants to acknowledge the fact that we are here for a limited amount of time. But the truth of the matter is that we only have a certain number of days to do something significant, legitimate or meaningful.

Yet so often, our time gets cluttered with worries, habits and distractions that keep us from experiencing everything God has in store for us. No matter how much time you have on earth, the great news is that God has a specific plan for your life. He has something in mind for you to do… to be… to accomplish.

Through this study, you'll discover how to shed the harmful thoughts and things that hinder you and steal away your valuable time. And you'll see how to get the most out of every moment.

God's best,

Ed Young

WEEK ONE

...NOT TO FISH

START IT UP

As many of you know, I love to fish. One of my favorite things about fishing is tying flies. When I am getting ready to tie a fly, I try to think about what the fish in that area want. I think about their feeding habits, their tendencies and anything else that might help me lure them.

A while back, a friend of mine invited me to his fishing lodge on Andros Island. Andros Island is one of the most remote areas in the Western Hemisphere. It has some fantastic fishing. So, before I went fishing I tied flies that matched what the fish were eating.

Today, I want you to do a little fishing with me. This fishing trip is going to have some powerful stuff in it. The fly is tied. I've got my gear and all my flies...let's go fishing.

1. Describe your first experience going fishing. What stands out the most about that experience and part did you enjoy the most.

_____

_____

_____

_____

...NOT TO FISH   LIFE'S TOO SHORT

TALK IT UP

Let's go fishing. That's what Jesus told a bunch of first century fishermen.

> As Jesus was walking beside the Sea of Galilee, he saw two
> brothers, Simon called Peter and his brother Andrew. They
> were casting a net into the lake, for they were fishermen. "Come,
> follow me," Jesus said, "and I will make you fishers of men."
> Matthew 4:18-19

This is a very unique text because Jesus was selecting his inner circle, his management team. Jesus could have chosen anyone. He could have chosen a bunch of farmers. He could have chosen a bunch of soldiers. He could have chosen a bunch of physicians or accountants. He could have chosen anyone, but seven out of the twelve he chose were fishermen.

2. If you were in Jesus' shoes today and needed to assemble 12 disciples, what types of people would you choose?

_____

_____

_____

_____

During this study, I am going to discuss with you some "fisheristics": characteristics that we all need if we are going to get in on the most powerful purpose in life—being a fisher of men. If you are not a follower of Christ, this study should show you how important you are. If you are a Christ-follower and you are already fishing, my hat goes off to you. And if you are a Christ-follower but not fishing, I don't want to bash you. I want you to realize how much God wants you to fish. So let's jump into the first fisheristic.

FISHERMEN HAVE *REEL* PURPOSE

Let's talk about the first fisheristic. We need to have reel purpose. The reason God does not zap us to heaven the moment we step over the line is because he wants us to bring as many people as possible into heaven. God has placed us in specific local bodies of water and he wants us to fish. We've got to get the purpose down because it will lead to the second fisheristic.

FISHERMEN HAVE *REEL* PASSION

When I take someone fishing who has never been fishing before and they feel the tug of the fish on the line, they get passionate. They are like, "Man, I've got to reel this fish in! This is cool! I like this!" They are passionate.

Jesus is passionate about fishing. He's passionate about those of us who know him personally, connecting with other people to communicate the life-changing message of the Gospel. He wants us to share in his passion.

> *Therefore go and make disciples of all nations, baptizing them in the name of the Father and of the Son and of the Holy Spirit...*
> Matthew 28:19

What part of "go" don't we get? Go and do what? "Make disciples of all nations." Notice the bookends of Christ's ministry. Jesus knew he only had about 36 months in the public domain, so what did he do? He picked fishermen. Why? Because life is too short not to fish. Then, three years after he invited disciples to go fishing, right before his ascension, he said "Go into all the world. Preach my Gospel. Baptize people."

So, Jesus started his earthly ministry talking about fishing and ended his earthly ministry on the same subject. Once we understand the powerful purpose, then we will have this "reel" passion.

Here's a major mistake that many Christ-followers make. Most of us see the Gospel as "God and me" instead of seeing the Gospel as "God and the world." We think, "It's all about me—what makes me look good, what fills my boat, what helps me, what feeds me. It's all about my growth and my maturity and me, me, me, my, my, my. God and me."

The problem is biblical Christianity is about God and the world. Scripture reads, "For God so loved the ... *world*," and, "Go into all the ... *world*." If we are not white hot with passion about reaching those outside of ourselves, then we are missing Christianity.

3. Why do you think so many Christ-followers don't share Jesus' passion for being a fisher of men?

_____

_____

_____

_____

Christianity is unique because Jesus tells me when I get outside of myself and think about others, that's when my needs are met. But when I get selfish and whiny and worry about me and mine, I have missed the good news. I've got to understand my purpose so I will share the passion of Jesus for those around me.

FISHERMEN HAVE *REEL* OPTIMISM

Something you will notice about fishermen is that they are optimistic. They're always saying, "We'll get 'em tomorrow." or, "That next spot, that next cove or that next flat—that's where we'll catch 'em." They take an optimistic approach and go where the fish are.

If we are going to truly go out into the world and reach people, we have to meet them where they are. When we go fishing, we think like the fish. So, when we fish for people we have to know how people away from the Lord are going to feel, what they are going to say, and how they are going to react to the Gospel.

A lot of people, though, when they go fishing, don't want to really get dirty or wet or slimy. They think, "Man, I don't want any part of that. It would be much easier for me to be kicking back at my house right now."

I believe Christians who are real fishers of men are not worried about getting a little slimy and even trying some different things. I'm talking about trying different flies, different lures, whatever it takes to catch the fish. And if one attempt doesn't work, they try something else. Christians should keep it up with an eternal optimism because you never know when the next cast could change someone's eternity.

That's why comfort doesn't cut it in God's economy. We can't just sit around and focus on our own comfort. We have to optimistically brave the elements to fish. We've got to try new stuff, we've got to be creative, and we've got to be innovative. Sometimes we will catch fish, sometimes we won't. But you know what? We don't worry about catching fish. All we are supposed to do is fish and leave the catching up to Jesus.

FISHERMEN HAVE *REEL* PERSISTENCE

Fishermen are persistent. They keep on fishing and because of that have story after story. If we will be persistent, we can tell about people who were cast to, reeled in and caught by the grace and power of God. So if you don't have any recent fish stories, you might be spending too much time in the marina.

Great fishermen keep on casting. You are not going to catch every soul. At Fellowship Church, we have many people that show up. They might connect a little bit, but they never take it. That's between them and God. Just because I lost some fish doesn't mean that I stop fishing. And just because someone doesn't accept doesn't mean we stop fishing.

Speaking of fish stories—there is this saltwater fish that is called a permit. They are brilliant fish which makes them hard to catch. Many people fish for twenty years and never even hook a permit.

I'm kind of obsessed with catching a permit. Well, two years ago my son and I were fishing in the Bahamas with our guide Prescott. While we were out, about a 25-pound permit ate my fly. I was freaking out.

I fought the fish for around an hour trying to reel him in. When the fish got close enough for our guide to grab him, something awful happened. The line popped and the permit swam away. I get teary just thinking about it.

4. If you have been fishing for very long, you have stories of ones that go away. Share some of your stories of people you have fished for that did not accept Christ?

...NOT TO FISH LIFE'S TOO SHORT

That was one of the worst days of my fishing life, but I didn't stop fishing. Once a year, my son and I go somewhere fishing in saltwater and I'm always thinking about the permit. Do you have fish stories? If you understand your purpose and understand the passion, then you are going to have persistence. You're going to be optimistic and come back with fish stories.

FISHERMEN HAVE A *REEL* PARTNERSHIP

Jesus never told us to be catchers of men. He says, "Just fish." You fish. You cast. You throw the Gospel out there. He will do the catching.

The apostle Paul described casting the gospel as planting a seed. When the Corinthian church was focused on who was making the seed grow (catching the fish), Paul wrote this.

> *I planted the seed, Apollos watered it, but God made it grow.*
> 1 Corinthians 3:6

5. How does this verse take the pressure off you when you go fishing?

_____

_____

_____

_____

One thing I have learned over the years fishing with my guide Prescott is that I always do better when I do exactly what he says. The same is true with life. If we do what the ultimate guide, our heavenly Father, says then our life is always going to go better.

But we have that tendency to try to do our own thing, to make our own cast. So often, I think the Lord shows us people to talk to or people to help. He puts them on our heart and sometimes we respond to it, and other times, sadly, we miss it because we are thinking about other things. We may be trying to do this deal, or make this amount of money, or chase this fun fix as opposed to really being sensitive and listening to what the Lord says.

We are partners with the Lord. The Lord is our guide. We've got to listen to him. We can partner with him once we step over the line of faith and receive Christ.

PARTNER WITH THE LOCAL CHURCH

We can also partner with the local church. The local church is the hope of the world. Jesus instituted and anointed one organization—the local church. We should be a part of a church and as we partner with the church, here is what we can do. We can go out and use our sphere of influence in our local body of water that God has given us. And, by God's grace and mercy, we can become fishers of men bringing people into the church.

A healthy church is a healthy body of water. A healthy church does not have just a bunch of big fat marlin swimming around in it. That is not a healthy church. A healthy church has three types of people, three types of fish in it. It's got some people, fish, who are going to hell. The second group of people are baby fish. They have been born again into the family of God and they are little babies. Then you have got the third group, a bunch of big fat marlin. If the big fat marlins are doing their job, then they are going out and inviting their hell bound friends to come to church. In turn, the hell bound friends are becoming Christ-followers and they are growing into what—healthy marlin.

One of the reasons Fellowship Church is so exciting is because we have adopted God's purpose—not mine, not yours, not the staff's—God's purpose. We go fishing and we are very passionate about it. We don't allow mission drift around here.

6. How have you partnered with your church to go fishing?

_____

_____

_____

_____

Everything we do is about fishing. Everything we do has a hook in it. Whether it's a song, a video, an activity, children's church, youth ministry, small groups or missions; they all have a hook. Because of that, we are partnering with the

Lord and he is empowering us to do this stuff. It's a miracle of the grace, the mercy and the energy of our fanatical fishing guide, God. We are in partnership with him.

WRAP IT UP

I kind of left you hanging with my permit fishing trip two years. I have been trying to catch a permit to make up for the loss, that tragedy when my line broke. Well, a year later I went fishing in that same area with Prescott and my son.

In that same area where I have the horrible memory of losing that permit, I hooked another permit. This time we were able to finish the deal and catch the fish. After I caught the fish, I didn't throw him in the live well of the boat. I practice catch and release so I released that beautiful permit back into the wild.

Think about the local church. Think about the people who have been reeled in by the grace, mercy and the power of God. Think about how we catch them and release them to let them grow, mature and become big fat marlin. It's incredible!

Jesus tells us to be fishers of men. Jesus will do the catching. All we do is fish. We cast and cast and cast. We cast by showing the love we have for others that comes from Christ. We serve them, help them, share with them and by tell them how we were caught by the hook of the gospel. That's how we fish. So, let's get started because life is too short not to fish.

Notes:

_____

_____

_____

_____

_____

LIFE'S TOO SHORT ...NOT TO FISH

Prayer Requests:

STEP IT UP

Take a step further over the next few days and spend some time reflecting on the following devotional thoughts that reinforce the previous session. Use these as reminders to take what you've learned and apply it to your everyday life.

DAY 1

Read James 4:13-14

If you know anything about fishing, you know that good fishermen will leave out early in the morning. It is still dark. It is calm and quiet outside. There might even be a fog on the water. If one wants to be successful in the fishing adventure, it pays to have the whole day available. Sincere fishermen don't sleep-in. They don't waste time hitting the snooze button. They don't wait until the sun is setting. Good fisherman make the most of all the time that is available in the day. Because they never know when they will get a strike and when it is time to try a different fishing hole.

Just like that morning fog on the water, time is evaporating on our opportunities to share the good news with others. James challenges us to make the most with what we have. Life is too short not to fish. Think about the time you were 'hooked' for Jesus. It was most likely because someone didn't waste time and went fishing. They casted and you took the bait. When I say 'bait,' I'm not talking about tricking someone into belief. I'm talking about communicating a message that they need to hear; something that will relate to them where they are, when they are there. Because when you do that, they'll be enticed enough to investigate further. And when they see the truth and power of who Jesus is, then he will hook them with his truth and power and life-changing message.

Spend this week reflecting on James' challenge. Pray for God's guidance for your life. Ask him to reveal his plans to you, that you may know his will.

Notes:

Prayer Requests:

DAY 2

Ephesians 6:19; Colossians 4:3; 2 Thessalonians 3:1

"Pray also for me...."

"And pray for us, too...."

"Finally, brothers, pray for us...."

These passages share something in common: the request for prayer. Most of us are asking others to pray for us, just as those are seeking our prayer for their lives. However, it is a different prayer request than many of us might be used to. These are risky prayers; bold requests. The authors of these passages are seeking opportunities. They desperately want God to open doors for them. Many of us are seeking open doors. We're looking for open doors in our careers, our business dealings, our personal relationships, our marriages and our finances. We're seeking opportunities for wealth, opportunities to close one more deal, opportunities to be healthier and opportunities for knowledge in our lives. How many of us are seeking those open doors to share the great wealth that is found in knowing Jesus Christ? When do we seek for the opportunity to bring life to those around us?

We are interacting with so many lives on a daily basis; it is shocking that we may go weeks, months and years without sharing how Christ has influenced our lives. In the above passages, the disciples were seeking prayer for themselves to share the gospel with others. They obviously had the right purpose identified and were focused on fulfilling that purpose.

Although we didn't walk side-by-side with Christ while he was here on earth, we share that purpose with the authors of Scripture: bring the good news to the world. Let's take our focus and put it on fulfilling God's will today—ask him to open doors for you to share the message of Jesus with someone. And once that door is open, that we "will fearlessly make known the mystery of the gospel."

> ***Have you had the door opened to a conversation with someone regarding God? Reflect on that situation and how God provided you the opportunity. If you haven't had that chance, continue to pray that the door would open.***

LIFE'S TOO SHORT ...NOT TO FISH

Notes:

Prayer Requests:

...NOT TO FISH LIFE'S TOO SHORT

DAY 3

Matthew 9:35-38

Good fishermen know how to spot circumstances for a potential great catch. Whether fishing in a lake, stream, river or ocean, there are usually areas for good fishing. Sometimes that circumstance is an uprooted tree that has fallen into the lake. Or a good circumstance might be that shady spot on the stream. A fisherman might spot that calm bend in the river, where the water is pooling, just right. Or maybe the tide has come in and that makes for good fishing. Each of these situations presents an opportunity to make a great catch. All the fisherman has to do is be on the lookout for these superior circumstances.

Most of our opportunities to share the good news are likely going to be with those people we know and love or those we spend the most time with each and everyday. A colleague or boss at work. A classmate or teacher. A business partner or customer. Perhaps even a child or spouse. Most of us aren't in the occupation of standing on the street corner, preaching. In fact, that is not what Christ is asking us to do. It is not the strangers who we should be seeking—the harvest is right under our nose, resting in those that are around us on a daily basis. And for the most part it is also not very likely that someone will just approach you and ask to be led to Christ. We need to be aware of the opportunities that God is presenting us with to share the gospel with others.

Jesus speaks about God needing more "workers into his harvest field." If a farmer were going to hire works for his field, he would seek many different skills, in order to produce a great harvest. Someone needs to plow the field, turning over the dirt and breaking up the rocks in the soil. Another needs to plant the seeds and someone else needs to tend to that seed—caring for it while it takes root. Finally, another harvests the crop at the proper time. Sometimes we will be the rock-breakers. Other times we will act as the planter of the seed. Even other times we will reap the crop.

Ask God today how you can be a worker in his harvest field.

LIFE'S TOO SHORT ...NOT TO FISH

Notes:

Prayer Requests:

...NOT TO FISH LIFE'S TOO SHORT

DAY 4

Isaiah 6:1-8

A good fisherman has a wide array of methods for catching fish. One method might be to us an artificial lure. There are many lures available to fisherman today. One type of lure might be something that mimics the behavior of something a fish would eat, like a fly or bug used in fly fishing. Another lure will be shiny in the water or make a sound that attracts the fish to it. There are even lures that have a particular smell that attracts fish. However, with all the technology and manufacturing of the artificial lures, there is nothing that beats live bait. Whether it is a worm, or a minnow, or squid, it seems that anyone can be a great fisherman with the right live bait. As fishers of men we have something similar to live bait in our tackle box. It is called "life-bait."

Isaiah shares a moment in his life when he witnessed the full glory of God, firsthand. Isaiah witnessed God, seated on his throne with angels surrounding him, singing praise. Fear gripped Isaiah, because he knew he was a man of sin and he could not stand in God's presence in such a state. In confessing his sin, Isaiah was instantly forgiven. And when God asked "who will be the messenger" Isaiah didn't hesitate to speak up and proclaim that he was ready.

Isaiah had experienced God's forgiveness and he was ready to share it with others. He had some serious "life-bait" in his tackle box to take to the people of Israel. God is putting that same life-bait in our tackle box. As a Christ-follower, we have an intimate relationship with God. We talk to him in prayer, we read of him in Scripture, we worship him through song. Many of us (if not all of us, let's be honest) have had those dark times in our lives and God was the light at the end of the tunnel. He got us through a financial crisis, a job loss or a marriage breakup. Maybe you have experienced humility in Christ. Or perhaps you are a poster-child for grace and forgiveness. Whatever your experience, you need to share these experiences with others—you need to use your life-bait.

__Pray for God to reveal how you can use the experiences in your life to share his love with others. Reflect on how others have influenced you by sharing their 'life-bait.'__

LIFE'S TOO SHORT ...NOT TO FISH

Notes:

Prayer Requests:

...NOT TO FISH LIFE'S TOO SHORT

DAY 5

Matthew 10:16-20

A fisherman's dream is making that trophy catch. Many fisherman believe that getting the trophy catch means being in the right place at the right time. Others might believe it has to do with having the best equipment. Imagine, as a fisherman, you have anything and everything available to you to catch the big one—the trophy fish. The line is right, the rod and reel are right, the bait, the location—everything is aligned for you to make that perfect catch. However, there is a simple truth about fishing. Even if you have the best equipment, the best lures, the best bait, all in the best boat, on perfect waters, at the perfect fishing hole... You...still...have...to...CAST. You have to put the line in the water.

Even if we don't know a lot about God's Word, we need to cast. Many of us get very fearful about talking to someone about Jesus Christ. What if they ask me to back it up with Scripture? What if I can't relate to that person? I haven't exactly been perfect around them, how can they take my word about Christ? None of our thoughts matter when we have the Creator of the universe on our side. In this passage in Matthew, Jesus is commanding the disciples about their purpose and what they can expect for following him. And when the time comes to speak—Jesus tells them that God will be their thoughts, that God will provide the words. Thankfully, we don't have to tell the perfect story or back it up with the perfect Scripture. God will do the talking for us. All we have to do is cast.

> ***Do you trust God with your thoughts and voice? As you are "casting," continually ask for God's thoughts and words to penetrate your own.***

LIFE'S TOO SHORT ...NOT TO FISH

Notes:

Prayer Requests:

WEEK TWO

...TO BE NEGATIVE

START IT UP

Stains can be a pain. Have you ever spilled coffee on your shirt and had to live with it for the rest of the day? Or maybe you dripped a little lunchtime salsa and soiled your shirt. Those spills can create great frustration. And in the end, we are left with dirty laundry.

Stains remind me of this week's subject matter, because negativity will soil your life. It will ruin a relationship, ruin a marriage, ruin a family, ruin a company, ruin a team, and it can even ruin a church. Life is too short to be negative, but there is something about us, something in our nature that loves dirty laundry. We like to sort through it, look at it, and hang it up for everybody to see—dirty laundry.

1. Try to name all the magazines and television shows that are dedicated to airing celebrities' dirty laundry.

_____

_____

_____

_____

Do you work with someone who always sees life like it is half empty? Maybe you are married to someone or live next door to someone like that. When you pull into your

27

church's parking lot and the parking crew directed you to a certain section, did you roll your eyes? When you run into an obstacle, do you feel like it always happens to you? If you answered yes to any of those questions, this lesson is tailor-made for you.

We are going to talk about how to negotiate, how to navigate around negativity. We are going to talk about how to get clean because a lot of us have this spot, this stain on our wardrobe called negativity.

TALK IT UP

When I say the word "negativity" what comes to mind? Negativity has many different nuances. Think about these words: slander ... gossip ... secrets ... sarcasm ... cynicism ... pessimism. If you say those words you will sound like a bunch of hissing snakes.

Negativity is all about those words. It disguises itself in different terms, but we love negativity. There is negative news. There are negative people. There is negative stuff in the sports world. The media is all about negativity. But before we point the finger of blame at the media, the media is simply a reflection of what we want. They are simply peddling what we like—dirty laundry, negativity.

Do you find yourself soiled? Do you find yourself wanting to get clean? Do you find yourself saying, "You know, I'm tired of this attitude. I'm tired of this demeanor that is messing me up and this propensity toward negativity. I can't really deal with it anymore." If that is how you feel, then this is the lesson for you.

CROSSED WIRES

A long time back, I drove a dilapidated Cherokee Chief. It was the third car I ever owned. This Cherokee Chief broke down all the time. It broke down so much that I had to carry jumper cables in the back seat.

One night I parked the Cherokee Chief beside my father's brand new, midnight blue Lincoln Continental. I got up the next morning and tried to start the Cherokee Chief, but it wouldn't start. I said to myself, "Okay, I'll just take out my jumper cables and use Dad's car to jump it."

LIFE'S TOO SHORT ...TO BE NEGATIVE

I jumped in Dad's car, pushed the release and the hood did that slow, mechanical lift—really fancy. I hooked up the jumper cables to his battery, then hooked up the jumper cables to my battery. I started his car and it was purring. I went to the Cherokee Chief and I began to rev the engine. To my horror, I watched the jumper cables catch on fire and melt into my father's brand new, midnight blue Lincoln Continental. It was terrible!

You know what happened? I got the wires crossed. I put the positive on the negative and the negative on the positive. And because I did that, we had a serious meltdown.

I thought about that while preparing this study because that is the problem in my life and that's the problem in your life when we go negative. We get the wires crossed, don't we? We put the positive on the negative and the negative on the positive and we have a meltdown. Life is too short to get the wires crossed. Life is too short to live in meltdown land. Life is too short to go negative.

2. How have you been burned by negativity; either by your own negative attitude or someone else's?

_____

_____

_____

_____

NEGATIVITY RUNS IN PACKS

Whenever I think about negativity, I think about a group of people who had their doctorate in negativity. I'm talking about God's chosen people, the Israelites.

They were miraculously delivered from Egyptian slavery. God parted an ocean so that they could cross on dry land. He guided them during the day by a cloud and at night with fire. He fed them manna burgers from heaven. He gave them an incredible piece of real estate. And right before they claimed the Promise Land, God did a quick time out and said, "Moses, choose twelve spies from the twelve tribes of Israel and have these people do a secret reconnaissance mission on the land that I am going to give you."

When the twelve spies came back, you won't believe what happened. These spies were well aware of all God had done to get them to the edge of the Promised Land, yet ten of the twelve spies had that dirty laundry mentality. Their wires were all crossed and they experienced a meltdown. Here's what they told Moses.

> They gave Moses this account. "We went into the land to which you sent us, and it does flow with milk and honey! Here is its fruit. But the people who live there are powerful, and the cities are fortified and very large...." Numbers 13:27-28

Negativity always runs in packs. You show me someone who is negative around your office and their friends will be negative too. Negativity breeds negativity. Ten out of the twelve spies went negative when they got back to Moses.

3. How have you noticed that negative people bring out negativity in you?

___

___

___

___

Why do we have this tendency toward negativity? Whenever I get lazy, I get negative. Whenever I say, "Well, I don't want to step up. I don't want to take the risk. I want to go ahead and play it safe." I get negative. Also, when I'm negative, I'm fearful. That's why I wrote a book called *Know Fear*. For about 300 pages, I talk about is the fear that we deal with and how to use it in a positive way. If we can deal with fear, we can get past negativity.

God told the Israelites, "Hey, I'm going to be with you. I'll give you the land. Go out and claim it." And God is saying the same thing to you and me. If we could see the real estate that God has in store for us, we would not believe it. Claiming it might look intimidating, but God is going to be with us. So, we don't have to get negative because God is with us.

NEGATIVITY IS INFECTIOUS

> *And they spread among the Israelites a bad report about the land they had explored. They said, "The land we explored devours those living in it. All the people we saw there are of great size. We saw the Nephilim there (the descendants of Anak come from the Nephilim). We seemed like grasshoppers in our own eyes, and we looked the same to them."* Numbers 13:32-33

If you think the flu and stomach viruses are infectious, those pale in comparison to negativity. Negativity is a highly infectious disease and it spread among the Israelites. Negativity, though, starts and stops with you and me. We might catch it from someone else, but we don't have to spread it. But what do we do? We just spread it because there is just something about dirty laundry that we like.

The ten negative spies spread a bad report. They began to exaggerate stuff. When I'm negative, when you're negative, what do we do? We exaggerate. "My waitress is taking forever! I've got a million things to do! I'll never get all this done! Oh, there's no way our company can do that. That client base over there, we could never penetrate that!" We exaggerate.

NEGATIVITY IS LOBBED AT LEADERS

The negativity of the ten spies became infectious. Before they knew it, the Israelites were infected and one of the key symptoms of negativity emerged.

> *All the Israelites grumbled against Moses and Aaron...* Numbers 14:2

It started with just the spies having a conversation with Moses, but it spread until all of the Israelites grumbled against who—Moses and Aaron. Whenever you lead, people will grumble.

4. How have you experienced people grumbling against you when you tried to lead?

_____

_____

_____

All of us are leaders in certain areas because leadership is all about influence. If you are a parent, you are a leader. If you are married, you are a leader. If you are a manager, you are a leader. If you are a coach, teacher or whatever, you are a leader. So get ready because if we are all leaders then that means people will grumble about you. So what do we do when it happens?

> ..."If only we had died in Egypt! Or in this desert! Why is the LORD bringing us to this land only to let us fall by the sword? Our wives and children will be taken as plunder. Wouldn't it be better for us to go back to Egypt?" And they said to each other, "We should choose a leader and go back to Egypt."
> Numbers 14:2-4

They were saying, "We'd rather be in slavery than here." Negativity always leads to slavery. It will become your master. You will become a slave to it and you will never get out of its bondage until you do what God wants you to do.

It's so sad. All of the Israelites who were in the moan zone, all of the Israelites who were into the dirty laundry thing, wandered in the desert for 40 years and did not get to enter the Promised Land. Their negativity kept them from God's blessing.

The Bible is so penetrating and powerful in its usage of negativity. It uses people who are positive and people who are negative to show us how to live. Jonah and Nehemiah are two people who lived on the positive end of the spectrum.

JONAH

Do you remember Jonah? God told Jonah to "go" to the evil city of Nineveh and tell them how sinful they are. Jonah responded by telling God "no" and hopping on a boat in the opposite direction of God's will. Jonah ended up getting swallowed by a fish then spit up back on land with a second chance. So Jonah went to Nineveh to preach and the entire city repented and turned toward God.

Now, you would think that Jonah would be giving people a high five, "Yeah! Oh, it was incredible! I was used by God in a great way!" Well, the Bible records that instead of that, Jonah was sitting on a hillside in the "moan zone." He was actually complaining that God didn't destroy the Ninevites.

Why did Jonah do that? He did it because, so often, we are negative towards

LIFE'S TOO SHORT ...TO BE NEGATIVE

others about the stuff that we have problems with in our own lives. The Ninevites had the same thing happen to them that happened to Jonah. They disobeyed, then God gave them a second chance. Jonah probably didn't like that, so he just began to rip them apart and cut them down.

It's amazing how negative we can be about something in another person's life when we have the same thing in our life. We need to learn from Jonah and avoid the moan zone.

5. What have you noticed in your life that causes you to go negative the most?

_____

_____

_____

_____

NEHEMIAH

We also need to learn from Nehemiah. When Nehemiah faced negativity, he did something we could learn from. Nehemiah was doing something that people said could not be done. He was rebuilding city walls around Jerusalem after they had been destroyed for over a hundred years.

While Nehemiah was organizing the Israelites to rebuild the city wall, others were going negative on him. They were cynical and pessimistic. So what did he do? He just kept building the wall. He didn't get down and try to argue with them. He kept to the vision God gave him.

We mess up when we chase down negativity. We are wasting our time. Don't think, "Oh, I better talk to this person at the office. They are saying this about me. I better talk to this person around the neighborhood. I better chase this person down." Do what Nehemiah did. Pray and stay above the fray. Stay at your task, stay at your purpose, stay at your goals, stay with God and he will take care of the rest.

6. What are things you could do to find encouragement and hope without chasing down those who are negative?

_____

_____

_____

_____

Maybe you're asking, "Well, Ed, is there any hope for me? I'm dealing with this negative person or I'm struggling with negativity in myself. I've got this stain on my wardrobe that I can't seem to remove."

Yes, there is hope for all of us because we can come clean. We can become pure before God.

CONNECT

"C" stands for connect. We've got to understand who we run with and connect with positive relationships. That means taking a long look at our relationships.

There are three types of relationships that most of us have. The first kind is the kind that will drain your battery dry. I truly believe Satan puts energy sucking people around every effective Christian because he wants to keep us neutralized and totally drained by these energy suckers. You can recognize them because when you seem them coming you think, "Oh, no. Not again. This person is going to drain my battery dry." We can't stiff arm everyone who drains us, but we have to be careful how many we keep around in our inner circle of relationships.

Another kind of relationship is with those people who are neutral. Neutral people give you some juice but they also take some away.

The third kind of relationship is like what I experienced Sunday afternoon—the replenishing re-charging, re-calibrating relationships.

After I speak Saturday and Sunday, I am drained emotionally. One Sunday I was tired and I felt down. So I called a friend of mine who is an encourager. After

LIFE'S TOO SHORT ...TO BE NEGATIVE

about fifteen minutes of talking to him I was feeling ready to go again.

Do you have replenishing people in your life? Do you have neutral people in your life? Do you have energy sucking people in your life? Is there a balance there?

7. Who are the replenishing people in your life and what makes them that type of person?

_____

_____

_____

_____

LOOK

"L" stands for look. We've got to look at the past, the present and the future. We've got to look at the past and what Jesus Christ has done for us. He died on the cross for our sins. He rose again! Also, look at the present. Take time to examine what he is doing in your life. Then, look at the future. Think about what he is going to do. The victory that the Bible promises should make every one of us positive. Every situation I face, I should look at the situation through God's eyes. We win. I'm going to live forever with the Lord.

ENJOY

"E" stands for enjoy. Enjoy what God has given you. Everything we have is a gift from God. And people who are spiritually mature realize that and appreciate what God has given them. They say things like, "God, I thank you for this breath I can take. I thank you just to be able to speak to others, to listen, to hear. I thank you for getting to be a part of a great church. God, I want to thank you. I want to enjoy the life you have given me."

You show me someone who is positive, and I'll show you someone who is thankful. Conversely, you show me someone who is negative, and I'll show you someone who is ungrateful.

ACT

"A" stands for act or action. We've got to activate our lives. We've got to do some positive things. For example, I've read that it takes ten positive statements to negate one negative statement. Isn't that wild? Do you remember negative stuff said about you? I do.

We remember negative stuff. It sticks to us like Velcro. That's the soil, that's the stain of negativity. To reverse it, as believers, we should be the most positive people out there. So, we should look to compliment and find the positive in every situation. Not false, phony baloney stuff. But the real stuff.

8. What could you do to help you see and communicate the positive around you?

___

___

___

___

NAVIGATE

"N" stands for navigate. We must to navigate through negativity. We can't navigate around negativity, but we are going to deal with negativity.

Here is something I have discovered about the Christian life. When God wants to build more patience in my life, do you think he puts me around patient people in patient situations? No. He takes me, this impatient guy, and puts me in situations that should cause impatience. Then, he asks me to defer to him and live my life doing the stuff I have talked about in Scripture. When I defer, he gives me the strength to use those impatient situations as a stepping stone, as a part of growing me.

So get ready. As you seek to be positive you are going to have lots of opportunities to be negative. But remember that God is using those as a tool to build us up so we can glorify him.

WRAP IT UP

Are you caught in the soiled and stained life of dirty laundry? It is time to let go of it and come clean. By God's grace and mercy, we can find the freedom and joy that comes from letting go of negativity. And in this short life we have, it is not worth being negative.

Notes:

Prayer Requests:

STEP IT UP

Take a step further over the next few days and spend some time reflecting on the following devotional thoughts that reinforce the previous session. Use these as reminders to take what you've learned and apply it to your everyday life.

DAY 1

Colossians 3:2

Life is too short to be toxic.

Have you ever noticed how one negative person can affect a whole group of people, often unknowingly? One person is negative to another, and that person is then negative to another who is negative to another. It is a vicious cycle that can be prevented.

Oftentimes we let worldly things get to us. Instead of focusing on all the positive God has provided for us, we focus on the negative and dwell on it. It can consume us and it can affect those around us. To avoid that negativity, Colossians tells us to set our minds on things above and not on earthly things.

"If you set your mind to it" the rest will follow. From an early age we are taught that if we focus on something and are willing to work to earn it, we will achieve it. The same can apply toward living a happy, positive lifestyle. If we want to be happy, we have to be willing to work for it. Focusing on God is not always easy, but the rewards are great.

Obstacles of negativity are always in front of us, but they are never above us. God is all things good. He is most high. When we look up with our hearts and really focus on God, he will always answer and guide our hearts with positive actions of influence.

How do you combat other people's negativity?

How do you combat your own negativity?

What are some ways you can make "looking up" part of your daily routine?

Notes:

Prayer Requests:

...TO BE NEGATIVE LIFE'S TOO SHORT

DAY 2

Jonah 3:10-4:5

When people change for the better, are we always happy for them? We know that our God provides mercy to his followers, and that mercy is something we celebrate and are thankful for when it is bestowed upon us. But if mercy is a good thing, why did Jonah become angry at the Lord's compassion?

If you think back to a time when you were a child, there was probably a kid, or maybe even a sibling, who you thought got away with everything. You knew though, that if you tried the same thing, you would surely be caught and punished. It probably didn't seem fair. That same attitude is what Jonah felt for God's compassion towards those he deemed "unworthy" of the Lord's forgiveness.

It's human to be selfish, to pass judgment and to want people to pay for their mistakes. But what if for every mistake you made, you had a crowd of tormenters who would follow you around town just waiting around to see how it was all going to catch up to you. How would you feel knowing that while you made a mistake, and were truly sorry for it, that those people were reveling in your downfalls and wishing bad things upon you because of your "history"?

God always has a plan for his people, the obedient and the disobedient. While you may feel that someone is getting away with something, remember that God cannot be deceived. He sees into the heart and reads the soul.

When God's grace is shown to those who on the surface may be viewed as undeserving, we should not doubt the Lord's intention. Only he knows what is truly on their hearts. We are called to be faithful and to believe that God knows best. He always has a plan.

> ***Describe a personal example of God's mercy in your life. What did you take away from that experience?***

LIFE'S TOO SHORT ...TO BE NEGATIVE

Notes:

Prayer Requests:

...TO BE NEGATIVE   LIFE'S TOO SHORT

DAY 3

Nehemiah 6:1-9

God has a plan for his work in each one of our lives. He calls us to answer him when he speaks. We are to faithfully follow no matter the obstacle or distraction.

Nehemiah shows us that people can be obstacles of distraction, intending to cause mental confusion and negativity toward a situation. This can make us question what we are doing and why we are doing it. When doing God's work though, we must remain focused. Increased awareness accompanied by prayer can help us recognize distractions and can also help us mitigate them.

Let's say you have a dream of starting your own company. You have a very clear vision of how you would like to run it and have developed a strong business plan that you are certain will be successful. You decide to share this vision with someone close to you and their response is "That's interesting, but it will never work." The very next day, you pitch your idea to an investor who you really need to help get your business started. Just as you finish your last sentence, he says, "I don't believe that's a good investment of my money." You are in disbelief. This plan was years in the making, you are a savvy business person and you know in your heart that this business would be a success. But the voices of these two people continue to repeat their negativity in your mind. What do you do?

Distractions can prevent God's work from happening, but only if you let it.

When in the face of a repetitive distraction, do not let yourself become worn out and do not lose focus. Always look distraction in the eye and give it the same response, "I do not work for you." Do not second guess what you are doing. If your hands become weak, pray for stronger hands. Continue to be the leader God chose you to be, showing a strong example for others to follow. Know that God's will be done because we work for the Lord and not for man. Have faith in that and his work will be completed.

> **Describe a time when negativity tried to influence your decision process. How did you combat it and what did you learn?**

LIFE'S TOO SHORT ...TO BE NEGATIVE

Notes:

Prayer Requests:

DAY 4

Hebrews 10:24-25

In today's society where so much negativity is in plain view for the whole world to see, it is easier than ever to develop a negative attitude or to be discouraged. To combat this, Hebrews tells to be constantly thinking about ways to motivate the spread of love, faith and service.

Interact. Encourage. Excite.

We all have our own unique God-given strengths and that is why our interaction with others is so critical. We need to do what we are called to do and use those strengths to the best of our ability. We are to serve God by serving others. To do that though, we need to *know* the needs of others. Meeting regularly is an easy way to accomplish this. Making yourself available for others and devoting your time to understanding their unique situations and circumstances will create a dialog that will let you know where you are needed.

When we share our trials with others, the burden can often become less, lightening our hearts. Talking through situations together can allow you to envision what it must be like to be in the other person's shoes and vice versa. It can also enable new visions of how to make a difference. Encourage those you speak with and let them know you are there for support. "For wherever two or more are gathered in my name, there too shall I be."

For every word of encouragement, smile, listening ear and pat on the back you give, God's favor is upon you.

How can you maintain a positive attitude in the face of negativity?

How do you motivate those around you in a positive, life-giving way?

LIFE'S TOO SHORT ...TO BE NEGATIVE

Notes:

Prayer Requests:

DAY 5

Ephesians 4:29

Words can heal as well as they can destroy. Words can be rocks or they can be a song.

Choose your words carefully. If you wouldn't want someone to say something to you, don't say it. We know that healthy words can lead to healthy relationships, but it's hard to always be positive; especially when someone's hurt your feelings or you have a very strong opinion about something. In these cases, it's helps to be selfless and think to yourself, "If Jesus was standing here, what would he say?"

Choose words to benefit and inspire your listeners. Our words should help build, encourage and lift up people. Jesus' time on earth was spent spreading the word of God. He was a teacher. In our own way, we are all teachers who have something to share with God's people. Our experiences make us who we are, and to that we all have a unique perspective that's never been heard before. Tell your story so that others may learn from it.

Choose to heal and not hinder. All of us deal with pain and hurt on some level. Some days, you're just having "one of those days". And then one person says something to you that strikes the final nerve and the rest of your day is shot. You go home in a foul mood and maybe it even spills into the next day. Don't be the person who says the words to set that cycle in motion. Think before you speak, and choose words of healing. It is something we all have the power to do. Help someone begin their healing process.

When in doubt, say unto others as you would have them say unto you.

Do you have a process for self-censorship and if so what is it?

LIFE'S TOO SHORT ...TO BE NEGATIVE

Notes:

Prayer Requests:

WEEK THREE

.....TO BE ENVIOUS

START IT UP

When I was five years old my mother looked at me and said, "Son, if you don't brush your teeth, you are going to end up having green phantom fangs." That made an indelible impression upon my life. Several days later, a photographer came by our home to take some pictures of the family. When the photographer smiled he had these green looking, pointy teeth. I remembered the warning from my mother and said, "Mom, he's got green phantom fangs!"

A lot of us have green phantom fangs—not in the dental world but in the relational world. A lot of us have the green phantom fangs of envy.

1. Describe a time you can remember being envious and what caused it?

_____

_____

_____

_____

Shakespeare called envy a "green sickness." When someone gets motion or sea sick we tell them they look green. It is an awful look. And when we are involved with envy, we are involved with a sin that is "u-g-l-y, you ain't got no alibi," ugly.

TALK IT UP

Envy is a sad sin when you think about it. At least other sins start off with some fun. Initially, when you are involved in pride, it feels kind of good to elevate yourself over another person. Anger can feel good in its initial stages. Envy though, starts out "u-g-l-y, you ain't got no alibi," ugly and it ends ugly. In fact, in the book of Galatians, it kind of details the running buddies of envy—and they are some pretty ugly dudes.

> *The acts of the sinful nature are obvious: sexual immorality, impurity and debauchery; idolatry and witchcraft; hatred, discord, jealousy, fits of rage, selfish ambition, dissensions, factions and envy; drunkenness, orgies, and the like. I warn you, as I did before, that those who live like this will not inherit the kingdom of God.* Galatians 5:19-21

2. Do you view some sins as more acceptable than others? Read the list of sins in Galatians again and determine which ones are considered "acceptable."

_____

_____

_____

_____

We may want to justify some sins in our lives. We may want to consider sins like envy as no big deal, but that is not how God sees it. Just look at the sins that envy is keeping company with. As I told you, the green phantom fangs of envy are bad.

It's obvious that envy is bad, but what is envy? Envy is being sad over someone's success or it's becoming a fan of another person's failure. Life is too short to be eaten up with jealousy, debauchery and all of this stuff that envy ushers in.

Well, what happens when we are envious? How does this stuff play out? What happens when we allow those green phantom fangs of envy to sink into our lives?

LIFE'S TOO SHORT ...TO BE ENVIOUS

ENERGIZED BY INSECURITY

Number one, we are energized with insecurity. Do you want to sign up for a lot of insecurity? Do you want the instability of finding your security in others? Just get involved in envy if you want those.

Psychology Today surveyed 25,000 adults who had a whacked out self-esteem. They discovered that people with a poor self-esteem were people who were eaten up by envy. Envy will energize insecurity. If I'm insecure, then I see myself the way you see me and not the way God sees me. A great self-esteem is seeing myself the way God sees me, nothing more and nothing less.

3. How have you seen insecurity related to envy?

_____

_____

_____

_____

You might think you have avoided the insecurity of envy, but what about camouflaged insecurity? You see this show up in transitional praise. Let me give you examples.

"Yeah, he's a good speaker, *but* is he the kind of guy you want to go fishing with?"

"She has a great physique, *but* have you seen her nails?"

"She is a great mom, *but* have you seen her house?"

But, but, but... Those are all signs of camouflaged insecurity and envy. And here's another way we camouflage envy—condescending comparisons. I'll never forget when it happened to me a couple of years ago when I bought a new truck. I was proud of this truck.

A guy asked, "Can I see your truck?"

51

I said, "Yeah."

He looked inside and said, "Man, this is a sweet truck, but it would look really cool if you tricked it out. What I would do is…" Then he went on to say, "If you want to see a real truck, my neighbor bought one and…."

Condescending comparisons—they are all about envy. That's why the book of Proverbs 27:4 boldly proclaims, "Who can stand before jealousy?" Do you want to sign up for some serious insecurity? Then you just allow envy to sink its green phantom fangs into your life.

ENVY DEVELOPS DISCONTENTMENT

Here's the second phantom fang of envy. Envy will develop discontentment in our lives. Our problem is that we are not content with our contents.

My mind rushes to Luke, chapter 15. It's a pretty powerful illustration. Jesus talked about the Prodigal Son. Let me give you the Cliff's Notes.

When the Prodigal Son was around 18 or 19 he took his Merrill Lynch trust fund, left his mansion and spent it on wild living. When he got to his last dollar he came to his senses, turned back, and went home.

His father greeted him, welcomed him home, invited his friends over, threw him this big party, and bought him a new wardrobe. This story is an awesome illustration of the grace and forgiveness of God. No matter how far we have gone, God waits and welcomes us back.

God's grace is definitely part of the story, but don't miss the subplot. My favorite part of the Prodigal Son story is the older brother. When he saw the leftovers and the clothes, he went on tilt.

Here is this older brother who was rolling in the "bling bling," living in the mansion, and driving his father's Range Rover and Lamborghini chariots. He had all this stuff at his disposal. But he was so mad about what he did not have. He was so envious of his brother that he missed thanking God and thanking his father for what he did have.

LIFE'S TOO SHORT ...TO BE ENVIOUS

> *The older brother became angry and refused to go in. So his father went out and pleaded with him. But he answered his father, "Look! All these years I've been slaving for you and never disobeyed your orders. Yet you never gave me even a young goat so I could celebrate with my friends. But when this son of yours who has squandered your property with prostitutes comes home, you kill the fattened calf for him!"*
>
> *"My son," the father said, "you are always with me, and everything I have is yours. But we had to celebrate and be glad, because this brother of yours was dead and is alive again; he was lost and is found."* Luke 15:28-32

4. How is the older brother's perspective flawed and how do we share his flawed perspective when we envy?

_____

_____

_____

_____

This happens in our lives when we get involved with envy. We are so focused on what we don't have and what is happening to other people that we miss the blessings of God. Envy is a bad deal.

ENVY SILENCES MY APPLAUSE OF OTHERS

> *Rejoice with those who rejoice; mourn with those who mourn.*
> Romans 12:15

Here's the third fang of envy: envy silences my applause for others. The Bible says we should applaud when others are blessed, but we don't do that when we are envious. We rejoice with those who weep and weep with those who rejoice. We do the opposite and it shouldn't be that way.

Ladies, what is your knee jerk reaction when your roommate rushes in ring

53

finger-high and shows you the ten-karat diamond she was just given? What is your knee jerk reaction when you know you don't have any prospects on the horizon? Guys, what's your knee jerk reaction when the guy you don't think is that smart closes some deal and makes 20 million dollars?

Whenever I am envious of someone else, I am trashing the grace of God. God is the one who gave them all the stuff. They might not realize it, but God is the one who has blessed them.

Do you remember King Saul? I call him, psycho Saul. He was tall, handsome, articulate and wired to be a great leader. He was on the battlefield one day in his tent, but he should have been out fighting the giant Goliath, a Philistine soldier. While Saul is hiding in his tent, this little Hebrew hillbilly, David, comes on the scene. David said, "I'll fight that giant."

Saul agrees to let David fight Goliath, but tries to give David his armor. The armor doesn't fit so David doesn't wear any. Instead, he goes to the river and collects five smooth stones as weapons against Goliath.

David was severely overmatched, but he won because God empowered him. The rest of the story is that the Israelites then dominated the Philistines. And after they had secured this incredible battle, the Bible says the Israelite army was marching back to J-town, I'm talking about Jerusalem. They were having a party and singing. The women began to sing "Saul has killed his thousands, but David has killed his tens of thousands! Saul has killed his thousands but David has killed his tens of thousands!" Saul heard it and went on tilt.

> *And from that time on Saul kept a jealous eye on David.*
> 1 Samuel 18:9

Saul was eaten up and eroded by envy. He was sad over David's success. Envy played a part in Saul's hydroplaning life. Life is too short to be envious. You don't want your life to be a tragedy of what might have been. Don't give in to envy and sign up for these things in your life.

ENVY GUTS THE GRACE OF GOD

Here's the fourth phantom fang of envy: envy guts the grace of God. In Matthew chapter 20, Jesus told a story. Jesus said a master hired all these people: he hired one at 6 am, another one at 9 am, another one at 12 noon, another one at 3 pm and another one at 5 pm. The master came back and paid the one he had hired last a full day's wages and also paid the one he hired first a full day's wages.

5. How would you have felt if you were the first person hired? How would you have felt if you were the last person hired?

_____

_____

_____

_____

Well, you can see where this story is going. The people who were hired first were like, "I can't believe it! I'm going to call an attorney. How about my rights?" They were moaning and complaining.

> "But he answered one of them, 'Friend, I am not being unfair to you. Didn't you agree to work for a denarius? Take your pay and go. I want to give the man who was hired last the same as I gave you. Don't I have the right to do what I want with my own money? Or are you envious because I am generous?'" Matthew 20:13-15

Are you envious because God is generous? Are you envious because that person looks that way, talks that way, sits in that office, uses that kind of transportation, lives in that size house, makes that kind of money, or has that kind of power? Are you envious because God is generous? Remember, it all comes from God.

You may be thinking at this point, "Wow, Ed, this is a pretty ugly discussion. I'm feeling down." I am, too. It's bad. Insecurity, discontentment, the inability to cheer people on, gutting the grace of God, not thanking God for stuff…is there hope for the envious?

Yes. We are all sinners. We all have a tendency to envy. Here is how we can turn envy's scowl into a smile. Here is how we can brush away the green phantom fangs of envy and turn it into a million dollar smile.

...TO BE ENVIOUS — LIFE'S TOO SHORT

GOD WILL SUPER-SIZE YOUR SECURITY

We need to come clean. We need to say, "God, I struggle with envy. I like to flare my green phantom fangs of envy." Once we do that, God will super-size our security. He wants us to see our security in him—nothing more and nothing less.

The moment I begin to worry about what you think, what you say, and what you feel, that's the moment my self-esteem turns horizontal. Our self-esteem should always be vertical. We should ask, "How does God see me? How is God looking at this?" That perspective will supersize our security.

GOD WILL CATAPULT YOUR CONTENTMENT

> *I am not saying this because I am in need, for I have learned to be content whatever the circumstances. I know what it is to be in need, and I know what it is to have plenty. I have learned the secret of being content in any and every situation, whether well fed or hungry, whether living in plenty or in want. I can do everything through him who gives me strength.*
> Philippians 4:11-13

I need to say, "God, I want to be content with my contents. You've given me this stuff, these abilities, and I am unique." When we come to God with our envy, he can exchange it for contentment not matter what our circumstance. So we need to see the unique things God has given us or even the unique way God has made us and appreciate it. Psalm 139:14 should help us appreciate our uniqueness.

> *Thank you for making me so wonderfully complex! Your workmanship is marvelous—how well I know it.*
> Psalm 139:14 (NLT)

We are God's workmanship." The word "workmanship" in the Hebrew means "poetry" or "poem." We are a piece of art. We are one of a kind. So, why compare yourself with others? When you compare yourself with others, you are making a mockery of God's creative genius. When God made you, he made you to be you.

6. How could you use Psalm 139 in a discussion with someone that is envious of another person's looks or abilities?

_____

_____

_____

_____

GOD WILL AMPLIFY YOUR APPLAUSE OF OTHERS

Here's the third thing that will happen when we come clean. God will amplify our applause. We need to learn how to rejoice with those who rejoice and weep with those who weep. When something good happens to someone else, realize it's from God. If they have a windfall, it's from God. Their ability to multiply is from God. That position is from God. We need to say, "Yeah, God!" That should be our mentality.

When you hang around certain people, do they rev up those envy engines? If they do, you better watch out how often you hang out with them. Driving through certain neighborhoods, does that rev up those envy engines? Do you say, "Wow, it must be nice?" Figure out when you are the most vulnerable to this aspect of envy so you can come clean with God and gain his strength over it.

GOD WILL BUILD UP YOUR BLESSINGS

Here's one more thing. When we come clean with envy, it will build our blessings. An earmark of spiritual maturity is how thankful we are. We don't need to let what someone else has freak us out about what we don't have. We need to thank God for what he has done in our lives. Thank God for his gifts.

That's why so many worship songs, so many Scripture verses, so much stuff that we talk about around here is about the "attitude of gratitude," this ability to live life like you are on a thank you safari. When I begin to thank God, I begin to understand what life is all about and envy begins to melt away from my life. This should impact our entire outlook.

We should be the most joyful people around, because we know Christ. We should be all about outrageous, contagious, excitement and thankfulness. We should say, "God, thank you. You are so awesome. Thank you for my life. Thank you for a roof over my head. God, thank you for my wardrobe. God, thank you for my position. Obviously you have placed me here for a dynamic reason and I want to give it back to you in the most developed way possible, as an act of worship."

WRAP IT UP

Are you green? Are you turning green with envy? Are you sad over someone's success? Are you a fan of someone's failure? Are you so freaked out about what you don't have because you are always looking at what other people do have? Drag envy into the light, because life is too short to be eaten up with envy.

Notes:

LIFE'S TOO SHORT ...TO BE ENVIOUS

Prayer Requests:

STEP IT UP

Take a step further over the next few days and spend some time reflecting on the following devotional thoughts that reinforce the previous session. Use these as reminders to take what you've learned and apply it to your everyday life.

DAY 1

Proverbs 14:30

You don't want it to happen, but sometimes it feels like you are powerless to stop it. You know it is not reasonable to feel the way you do, but justification and rationalization can have little effect. As you stand admiring the blessings of others, that aching sensation deep within you grows stronger. It is envy and it is a formidable foe.

You know that rotting feeling. "Why doesn't something like that ever happen to me?" "They don't deserve that as much as I do!" "When is it going to be my time for something like that to happen?"

The agony of those pestering questions can make you lose sleep, lose focus and lose a life a peace. Envy is a dangerous game and the worst part is, there is no winner. The person you envy doesn't experience your agony. And as long as you continue in the envy game, you will never win either.

Don't let envy become an uncontrollable force in your life. God can give you the strength to overcome this poisonous emotion. Every time you feel envy start to well up inside of you, identify it for what it is. Admit that it is envy and go to God with that problem.

> *Pray that God will overcome the envy within you. Then, ask God to help you appreciate what he has given you.*
>
> *Identify an area that you are struggling with envy.*
>
> *Ask God to show you why you are envious. Then, ask God to show you what you have to be thankful for.*

LIFE'S TOO SHORT ...TO BE ENVIOUS

Notes:

Prayer Requests:

DAY 2

Proverbs 23:17

What do you envy?

What you envy is a sign of what you desire. If you find yourself envious of your old drinking buddies because they still get to go out and party like you once did—that is a sign of your desires. If you are envious of the way your non-Christian friends freely spend their money—that is a sign of your desires.

What we envy can tell us a lot about who we are. It reveals the deepest desires that we might not act on, but they still direct our lives. Those passions reveal what we truly think is best. And if we are envious of a life of sin, that tells us something about what our priorities and commitments are.

If you find that you desire things that sin against God, you can't just try to subdue those desires. You can beat them down and push them back, but they will rear their head again. The answer is to replace those desires. Put your effort into pursuing God and his passions. Become deeply committed to the things of God and notice how God can transform your desires.

How could you pursue the desires of God this week?

LIFE'S TOO SHORT ...TO BE ENVIOUS

Notes:

Prayer Requests:

DAY 3

Galatians 5:24-26

When we belong to Christ, we will live differently—not perfectly, but differently. Before Christ, we lived according to the sinful nature whether we realized it or not. We called the shots and our decisions were founded in the sin nature that we all possess. So even with our best attempts, we came short of what God intended for us.

Then came our encounter with Christ; that day when we realized we were controlled by something destructive and degenerate rather than the righteous freedom that Christ offers. So we confess our sin and admit our need for Christ. The result is we find new life in place of all that previously existed.

So when the temptation to return to what was knocks on our door, we can turn back to the Spirit. We can find hope and healing for our sin as the Spirit produces what we could never produce.

Read Galatians 5:22-23 and ask God to crucify your sinful nature and produce the fruit of the Spirit in your life.

LIFE'S TOO SHORT ...TO BE ENVIOUS

Notes:

Prayer Requests:

DAY 4

Colossians 2:6-7

"Overflowing with thankfulness." That is an incredible phrase. Imagine a life that is so full of thankfulness it is literally flowing out because it can't be contained. There is a new level of experience in life as the beauty of each moment is appreciated instead of ignored. There is a new depth to each encounter as the best is recognized and admired. The life overflowing with thankfulness is some extraordinary, yet how many of us live it?

It is so much easier to be consumed with what we do not have than to be enthralled by what we do have. There is always a bigger house, nicer car, better office and larger bank account. But chances are, if you were to list the things you value most, those things I mentioned would not be included. You would list things like good health, family and friends. You would discover what truly makes you happy is much simpler than what you strive for.

The irony of envy is we become consumed with pursuing what we think will fulfill us instead of being fulfilled with what we already have. The envious pursuit leaves us empty while the life of thanksgiving causes us to overflow.

Exchange emptiness for overflowing. Trade in envy for thankfulness. You can do this by learning to appreciate the simplest things. Thank God for the cool breeze, the green grass and the blue sky. Then push further. Thank God for creating you with the ability to feel the cool breeze, and distinguish between the lush green grass and brilliantly blue skies. Or how about thanking God for the ability to not only notice, but enjoy those things?

There is a world worth being thankful for if we take the time to appreciate it. When we take the focus off what we don't have and put it on what we do have, we can move from the emptiness of envy to and overflow of thankfulness.

Spend five minutes thanking God for things in your life.

LIFE'S TOO SHORT ...TO BE ENVIOUS

Notes:

Prayer Requests:

DAY 5

James 5:16

Have you heard of a "gateway drug"? The idea is that some drugs lead to others. For example, someone might start smoking marijuana because they think the effects are manageable, but the desire for that high leads to experimentation with other drugs. Before the person knows it, the drug they started with opened them up to a world of drugs they never thought they would get to.

James is warning that envy and selfish ambition are gateways to much worse things. We might think being envious only hurts us, but that is not true. Our envy will reach out and touch others. In James' warning, it leads to "disorder and every evil practice."

How? Envy and selfish ambition put the focus on us. We become consumed with our own desires and that will lead to elevating ourselves above others. The result is that we put our wants above the needs of others and do whatever it takes to satisfy ourselves—even to the point of harming others.

Jesus said all the Old Testament commands and warnings could be boiled down to loving God and loving others. When we love God, we put him as the focal point. And with God as the focal point, we are not longer just focused on how to satisfy our needs so we are free to love others.

> ***Ask God to help you identify the source of your envy and what you can do to overcome it.***

LIFE'S TOO SHORT ...TO BE ENVIOUS

Notes:

Prayer Requests:

WEEK FOUR

...TO BE SELFISH

LIFE'S TOO SHORT

START IT UP

It's said that monkey trappers in the Far East have an interesting technique for catching monkeys. They take a pumpkin gourd and carve a small hole in it to carve out the inside. Then, they take a piece of fruit, like a banana, and put it inside the gourd. Finally, they stake the gourd to the ground and wait.

The trappers count on the curiosity of the monkeys to bring them to the gourds. The monkeys will put their hands inside the gourd to get the piece of fruit, but once they grab the fruit their clenched fists are too big to pull back out. The only way they can get their hand free is to let go of the fruit and slide their hand out the same way it went in.

The monkeys trap themselves. And when the trappers walk up, the monkeys still won't let go. The monkeys could have freedom if they would just open their clenched fists and release the fruit. But they keep a tight grip on their prize and end up losing their freedom.

1. What's something you have unwisely held on to that has cost you?

_____

_____

_____

_____

71

TALK IT UP

One man gives freely, yet gains even more; another withholds unduly, but comes to poverty. Proverbs 11:24

One man is open-handed. The other man is close-fisted. One man is a giver. The other is a grasper. One man has his eyes on those around him. The other man is looking just at himself. The result is these two men have very different outcomes.

Life is too short to be selfish. We don't want to be the close-fisted, selfish person. God wants us to experience the freedom of having open hands and giving generously. If we want to experience the freedom of letting go of selfishness, we need to take a hand exam.

CHARACTERISTICS OF BEING OPEN-HANDED

Generosity

The verse we read earlier says, "One man gives freely." That gives you the first tell tale mark of an open-handed person—generosity. They are generous with their time, words, possessions and finances. When someone is in need, they volunteer to help. When the church has a need, they step up their giving. When they notice a person having a bad day, they offer a kind word. Open-handed people give freely.

Abundance

Generosity leads to the second tell tale mark of an open-handed person and you see it again in the verse from Proverbs. "One man gives freely, yet gains even more." In other words, open-handed people have an abundance.

It's natural to think that when we are giving things away, sooner or later we are going to run out. But that's not how it works. The Bible says that when you and I are willing to give, God will continue to give to us. In fact, those who are open-handed have discovered a powerful dynamic in the Bible. We will never be able to out-give God.

Luke 6:38 records Jesus' words, "Give and it will be given to you." That same principle is at play when the Bible says, "One man gives freely, yet gains even more." It continues to come back to him so that he always has an abundance; he always has what he needs. But in the midst of giving, it's rolling back to him. The open-fisted person learns that God cannot be out-given.

Confidence

Generosity comes with a third sign—confidence. Confidence comes from a long, established track record with God. You've learned that you can't out-give God so you are confident to give because you know God will provide for you.

After a while, you begin to realize, "I really can be confident about tomorrow and the day after and the day after because God will always provide for me." An open-handed person realizes God is his provider so he can relax and trust God. His confidence is in God and not his own abilities to make ends meet.

2. Describe an area where you have built a track record with God that has produced confidence?

___

___

___

___

If you examine your life and notice generosity, abundance and confidence, then you could be an open-handed person. But, on the other side of an open-handed person is a close-fisted person and they have tell tale signs as well.

CHARACTERISTICS OF A CLOSE-FISTED PERSON

Stinginess

The verse we read from Proverbs talks about a second kind of person and that is the close-fisted person. "Another man withholds unduly." Stinginess is the first tell tale sign of being close-fisted. A close-fisted person is cheap, a penny pincher and a hoarder. Their philosophy in life is, "Get all you can, can all you get, sit on the can, poison the rest."

They are cheap. They are that way toward their family. They are that way toward their friends. They are that way even toward their church. They are cheap with what they have. They are cheap with their time. They are cheap with their words. They are cheap with their finances.

Stinginess is the characteristic of their life because they have got this idea that, "If I can just hoard everything, if I can just get more and hang on to it, I'm going to be okay. It's going to be alright. Tomorrow's going to be a better day."

3. What are you the most tempted to be stingy with?

_____

_____

_____

_____

Lack

The irony of the stingy mindset is the second characteristic of a close-fisted person. A close-fisted person lacks. It's described in Proverbs. "Another man withholds unduly, but comes to poverty." In other words, there is a constant lack in his life.

He's the kind of individual that every time he takes a step forward, he takes two steps back. And after a while, it begins to dawn on him, "Whoa, time out! I'm not getting anywhere. In fact, I keep going backwards. The tighter my hands get, the more I hoard things, the more I jam it into my little can, it doesn't get better. It gets worse. I see lack in my life more and more."

The close-fisted person thinks they finally have everything in order. And then the refrigerator breaks. Or an unusual bill pops up. Then the dog has to go to the vet. It's one thing after another that keeps taking from them. It's like a siphon just sucking things away and it never stops.

Anxiety

It's no wonder that close-fisted people have this third characteristic—anxiety.

LIFE'S TOO SHORT ...TO BE SELFISH

They keep seeing their treasured time, possessions or finances slipping away. "Are we going to have enough? Are we going to be able to pay this bill? Are we going to be able to do this? Can we go here? Can we do that?"

Those who are close-fisted have their eyes focused on what they can do and only trust in what they can do. If that's you, you've got every right to be worried. We don't even know what the next five minutes is going to bring. So think about it, how can we trust ourselves to provide for every one of our needs when we don't even know half the needs we will have.

4. As heavy as the weight is trusting ourselves, why do you think so few people exchange that weight for trusting God to provide?

_____

_____

_____

_____

So how did your hand exam go? Are you an open-handed person? Are you a person characterized by generosity that leads to abundance that leads to confidence? Or are you close-fisted, characterized by stinginess, lack and anxiety?

If you are an open-handed individual, keep doing what you are doing. You haven't even begun to see what God can do. But if you are discovering that you are more close-fisted than open-handed, you need a hand exchange.

EXCHANGE STINGINESS FOR GENEROSITY

But just as you excel in everything—in faith, in speech, in knowledge, in complete earnestness and in your love for us—see that you also excel in this grace of giving. 2 Corinthians 8:7

We need to learn to become excellent givers. We need to exchange our stingy practices with generous ones. We need to learn how to and the only way to learn it is to give.

By the way, learning generosity is not about how much money you have. I meet people who tell me, "You know, I really don't have that much now so it's tough to be generous. But when I get more, I'm going to learn to be generous." The problem is, if you are a poor tightwad and you come into money, you're just going to be a rich tightwad.

If you are a Christ-follower, do you understand that the Spirit of God lives within you? You have the very Spirit of God, who intimately knows the heart of God, living in you. And do you know what God's heart is? God's heart is to give.

One of the most famous verses in the Bible is John 3:16 and it describes God's heart of giving. "God so loved the world that he gave..." Because of God's Spirit in you, you are wired to give. And when you refuse to do that, you are putting on the brakes of who you are meant to be. No wonder you are feeling frustration in your life. You are acting contrary to the Spirit of God inside you.

If you are not a Christ-follower, God wants to start with being generous to you. He gave his very Son so you could experience his love. He paid the penalty of our sin and brings us into a relationship with him. And when we accept the gift of love and forgiveness that God has offered us through Jesus, God will place his Spirit in us. Then we can extend the generosity that God has shown us.

So if we want to be generous, we follow God's example and start giving. A great place to start is giving to your friends and family. Take them out to eat and pay for it. Then watch what happens because of your generosity. Then, if you want to continue to excel in giving, give a generous tip to the waiter! You're not going to learn how to be generous until you do it.

5. What is something generous you could do this week?

_____

_____

_____

_____

EXCHANGE LACKING FOR ABUNDANCE

When we begin to excel in giving, we move from lack to abundance. We will experience God's abundance and realize we cannot out-give God.

> *Remember this: Whoever sows sparingly will also reap sparingly, and whoever sows generously will also reap generously.*
> 2 Corinthians 9:6

We reap what we sow. If we are a cheap, penny pincher when it comes to sowing, we shouldn't expect to get back generous amounts. But if we're a generous giver, we will reap generously.

And I tell you, sometimes I wish I could just slide in beside people. I wish I could tell you just how real this is. This really does work. These are not just words in a book. This is a dynamic that comes into play when you begin to trust God. So take this seriously and begin to be excellent givers, and you will see this dynamic working in your life.

You might be thinking that is something that only works for pastors or people who have some special relationship with God, but that is not true. The principle of God being generous works when we take seriously the Word of God and learn to be excellent givers. And as we do, we put into play this dynamic that those who sow generously will reap generously from God.

Now, I know I will sow when I reap, but I don't give to get. Don't fall into that trap. I give because that's the heart of God. But I also know that God is going to give back. He tells me so in his Word. And I also have learned over many years, I can never ever out give him. And when you learn to be generous givers; when you learn to open your hands up; when you stop living close-fisted, but open them up, and excel in giving, you will see lack move to abundance. And as you do that, then you will move from anxiety to confidence.

EXCHANGE ANXIETY FOR CONFIDENCE

> *"Therefore I tell you, do not worry about your life, what you will eat or drink; or about your body, what you will wear. Is not life more important than food, and the body more important than clothes? Look at the birds of the air; they do not sow or reap or store away*

in barns, and yet your heavenly Father feeds them. Are you not much more valuable than they?" Matthew 6:25-26

"But seek first his kingdom and his righteousness, and all these things will be given to you as well." Matthew 6:33

If we will seek the kingdom of God and God's righteousness, Jesus promises that all the things that we need will be there. God will provide.

6. How have you experienced God provide for you when you put his priorities first?

_____

_____

_____

_____

Well, what does it mean to seek the kingdom of God? Put God in his proper place in your life. That expression "kingdom of God" means the reign or the rule of God. It means that you and I get to the place where we recognize, "I'm not in charge. God is. God rules over my life. He is for me, not against me. He loves me with a love that I can't even begin to understand and I submit my life to his rule, his reign, in my life."

Then as I do so, I seek his righteousness, or more literally, his right way of doing things. What is God's right way of doing things? It is explained in the Bible. There are dynamic life principles that need to be implemented. When we actually begin to obey the Word of God, when we put him in his proper place, when we begin to live life his right way, he will take care of all the rest.

THE TEST OF THE TITHE

There are lots of basic principles in the Bible, but there is one that I have found that is really where the rubber meets the road. It has to do with something that is near and dear to all of us—our finances.

> *"A tithe of everything from the land, whether grain from the soil or fruit from the trees, belongs to the LORD; it is holy to the LORD."*
> Leviticus 27:30

The word "tithe" means one tenth, 10%. God was saying to the nation of Israel in Leviticus, "One-tenth of everything you produce, whether it is from your trees, from the grain of the ground, or even the animals that are not mentioned here," God says, "The first ten percent of any income or gain belongs to me."

Now they were living in an agricultural economy, so obviously it was coming from the fruit of the trees, the grain from the ground or the animals that they raised. Well, you and I are not living in an agricultural economy in the same way. What God is saying to us is, the first ten percent of all income or gain belongs to him.

God doesn't need our money. But when you and I learn to bring the first dime out of every dollar to God through the church, we are acknowledging in a very practical and tangible way, "God, I put you in your proper place in my life. I trust you."

I can hear some of you going, "Whoa, whoa, whoa, time out. I can't afford to do that." Guys, listen to me. I can't afford not to. Not because God is going to come down and beat me up. But I don't want to miss out on all the blessings God will pour out. We will miss out on this if we keep a tight fist towards God.

WRAP IT UP

Which do you want? What kind of hands do you want? It's all about the hands. Do you want to live close-fisted? That's your call. But that's not really a way to live.

God says if we will open our hands and learn to be excellent givers, he will always cause more to come back. And, we will live a life of confidence because we will have a very positive outlook on life. Life is way to short to live selfishly and to live close-fisted. Let's open our hands.

...TO BE SELFISH LIFE'S TOO SHORT

Notes:

Prayer Requests:

STEP IT UP

Take a step further over the next few days and spend some time reflecting on the following devotional thoughts that reinforce the previous session. Use these as reminders to take what you've learned and apply it to your everyday life.

DAY 1

1 Peter 4:9-10

If you have a talent, let it be seen.

God has blessed each of us with various talents, and what we have to offer is uniquely different from the people around us. Talents and blessings should not be taken for granted, because each is given for a reason.

God does not bless us to watch our talent go to waste.

If we view our talents as blessings, or Godly challenges to see just how far we can take them, we can catch a glimpse of God's plan for the future—a world where all of his children are working for and serving him. It may be difficult to imagine, but what if that world did exist, and you had the opportunity to be a part of it. How far would you want your talents to go?

The Bible tells us that we should generously use our gifts for service, and to offer that hospitality without complaint. We might face times when we know that we could add value to a situation, but might choose not to because we might feel we have something better do or maybe are just worn out from a day's work. It's important to remember that the Lord's work is never done, and we are important conduits to that.

We are challenged to use our gifts as faithful servants. For Christ followers, sitting on the sidelines is not an option. God calls us to follow in Jesus' footsteps and to serve. To serve literally means to render obedience. In our obedience to God, we are to do His will and offer our talents and service wherever they are needed.

Blessings can be filled with happiness, but if we are not using our talents, are we truly experiencing the happiness that God has planned for us?

LIFE'S TOO SHORT ...TO BE SELFISH

What talents do you have that you can offer up in service?

What talent will you commit to begin using today that you feel can really help make a difference? How will you use it?

Notes:

Prayer Requests:

...TO BE SELFISH LIFE'S TOO SHORT

DAY 2

Romans 12:13

God has a lot of work to do. That is why he entrusts us with the important task of sharing ourselves with those in need. What a blessing to be chosen by God to do His will.

Practicing service is one of the many ways we can serve the Lord. We are made in God's image and likeness, and when we share ourselves with others, a part of God within us is passed on to those around us.

The fast paced world we live in may often consume many hours of our time, but there's always a second to step back. Even what little we can do is needed and appreciated. While we may not always feel like opening our hearts, time and resources, remember that each of us are in demand. Whether we feel like dedicating ourselves or not, we are still being called to serve.

When we take the time to step back and look at all of the need outside our bubble, we can see that there is opportunity everywhere. All of God's children need to be loved and cared for, and every day is an opportunity to change someone's life. Even a few seconds of effort can turn into someone's smile.

You can choose to spread yourself thin, or you can spread yourself thick by consciously choosing daily activities that are heavy in righteousness. Choose to make an impact today and let people know that you are here.

Remember a time when someone wasn't a servant to you, but you wish they had been. How did that affect you?

What new ways will you choose to be a servant today?

LIFE'S TOO SHORT ...TO BE SELFISH

Notes:

Prayer Requests:

DAY 3

3 John 1:5-8

Go beyond the traditional, and do something innovative.

Our faith in God can take us beyond the traditional ways of giving.

Just as Jesus carried the cross for us, we too should be willing to walk the extra mile to find all the undiscovered, less talked about, maybe even less desirable ways to make an impact in giving. You can never tell when going the extra distance will allow you to extend your faith to you'd never imagined.

Strangers or not, we're all brothers and sisters, and as family we're called by our Father to help each other out. There are so many stories waiting to be shared from your good work, and today is a good time to start.

Think about a time when a perfect stranger helped you out of a situation. A time when you thought to yourself, "Wow, if they hadn't done that for me, I don't know what I would have done." Now take that instance and think back to all the people you told about it. Whether you knew it or not, because of that one person, you were spreading God's good news. Someone heard your cry, you were graced and your prayer was answered.

God's work was done that day.

> **What hinders us from thinking out of the box or being more free givers? What are some ways to combat those ideas?**
>
> **What are some ways you'll seek to go beyond the traditional ways of giving and generosity?**

LIFE'S TOO SHORT ...TO BE SELFISH

Notes:

Prayer Requests:

DAY 4

2 Corinthians 9:6-15

Providing for people in need is a way of giving thanks for what we have been given. It's like silently saying, God has blessed me and He has asked me to share that with you.

As we open our hearts to God's will, everything we do for others is obedience for God's glory. God loves a cheerful giver, one who gives freely and without hesitation. When we give unselfishly, we are demonstrating our faith. As we provide for others, he too will provide for us.

Paul tells us in 2 Corinthians that if we are generous, God will return the favor. When we sow, we scatter God's blessings for growth. When we reap, we harvest those blessings. Reaping and sowing are a unified, continuous process that requires diligence from beginning to end.

When we scatter our blessings to others, God hears their prayers of gratitude as they have been encouraged and excited by faithful servants. The hearts you touch, even with the smallest of gestures, speak happily of your name because you were there when God asked you to be.

It's reassuring to know that if you are obedient to God's will and you share what you have with others, you will be provided with all you need, every time you need it.

Why do you think the words "all" and "every" appear so frequently in this passage?

What do you think is the significance of the phrase "every man should give what he has in his heart decided to give"?

LIFE'S TOO SHORT ...TO BE SELFISH

Notes:

Prayer Requests:

DAY 5

Psalm 37:25-26

God knows that being generous is not always the easiest of tasks. It can require us to put others first, even when we feel like saying, "What about me?" Generosity is a challenge. We don't naturally want to give. But God gives us opportunities to realize that we each can influence the world.

Living generously in God's world of giving requires big commitment and trust. In this case, committing to the Lord is giving to the cause of others, no matter what the cost. And trusting is following through with our faith, knowing that if we do what is asks, he will fulfill his promises. God always provides us the means to be generous, but does that generosity always make it to its end?

Psalm reminds us that if we give generously, we will always be taken care of. The righteous will never be forsaken, and our future generations will be blessed if we choose to live with a generous spirit. That knowledge can serve as the power to "just do it" when it comes to giving. When all is given for his glory, God will remember you when you need him, and he will not let you fall. Faithful servants do not go unnoticed.

All generosity happens for a reason. God has begun work within you that he intends to see through. When you say "yes" and aid him with unselfish good deeds, the rewards are great. Work that God has started within you will always be finished and will always be rewarded.

If God can just give people whatever it is they need, why are we called to fill the needs of others ourselves?

LIFE'S TOO SHORT ...TO BE SELFISH

Notes:

Prayer Requests:

WEEK FIVE

...TO LIE

START IT UP

It's amazing how many things that we run into everyday that have layers to them. Have you ever thought about that? We constantly see stuff that has layers, but many times we don't think about the layers.

For example, think about our skin. We have the epidermis, the dermis and the hypodermis layers of our skin. We normally don't think about it, but our skin has a bunch of layers. Or, what about sushi? The California roll has a bunch of layers to it. It's got rice, seaweed, avocado and crab layers. Then there's the baseball. A baseball has layers to it—leather, yarn, rubber and cork. Our beds have layers—comforter, blanket, sheets, mattress pad, and mattress. It's really amazing when you think about all the layers of stuff.

Today I want us to talk about the layers of something that is intangible; but this intangible thing has some very tangible consequences in our lives. I want us to think about the layers of lies we tell.

Many people are living under layer after layer of lies. Don't you hate to be lied to? When someone lies to me I feel violated, don't you? I feel taken advantage of. I hate it when people lie to me.

It's kind of hypocritical though. On one hand, we hate being lied to. But on the other, we don't mind lying when we need to. It almost seems like we are expected to lie when the heat is on.

...TO LIE LIFE'S TOO SHORT

1. What's the most off-the-wall lie you have ever told or been told?

_____

_____

_____

_____

TALK IT UP

There are six things the LORD hates, seven that are detestable to him: haughty eyes, a lying tongue, hands that shed innocent blood, a heart that devises wicked schemes, feet that are quick to rush into evil, a false witness who pours out lies and a man who stirs up dissension among brothers. Proverbs 6:16-19

If you are a scorekeeper, you'll see that two of the seven things in this passage of Scripture have to do with verbal dishonesty. That should help us realize the severity of this sin.

We justify our lies with classifications like "white lie." No matter what color we give it, God still sees our lies as a serious problem.

As I said earlier, we hate to be lied to, but we don't mind lying when we need to. As much as we hate being lied to, God hates it even more.

NATURAL BORN LIARS

No one taught me how to lie. I just know how to lie. And I'm good at it. I just know how to tweak the truth and so do you. And if you have children, you know that nobody has to teach them how to lie.

When my son, EJ, was three years old, he hit his sister LeeBeth in the arm. LeeBeth ran to me and said, "Dad, Dad, EJ just hit me in the arm! Look."

There was a big whelp on her arm so I called in EJ. I asked, "EJ, did you hit

LIFE'S TOO SHORT ...TO LIE

your sister?"

He said, "No." He looked me square in the eye and just lied. "No, Dad."

Then I got smart. I used some psychology on him. I said, "EJ, where did you hit your sister?"

He said, "Right there on the arm."

Now, I didn't teach him that. He's a natural born liar. I'm a natural born liar. You're a natural born liar. So, let's just be honest, we're all liars.

We are all living under layers of lies and a lot of us don't even realize it. I want to bring the layers out into the open because I want us all to understand the greatness that God has for our lives. That greatness involves the freedom of the truth. In fact, Jesus said, "Then you will know the truth, and the truth will set you free." (John 8:32)

LAYERS OF LIES

Let's get to the freedom that God has for us by putting some labels on the layers of lies.

The Elevation Layer

The first layer has to do with elevation and plays itself out in things like padding your resume or name dropping when you don't really know the person. It can be tempting.

2. Why do you think we are so tempted to lie by elevating our past experiences or accomplishments?

_____

_____

_____

_____

I had lunch with an NBA player and we were talking about my basketball career at Florida State University. There was something inside of me that wanted to elevate myself and my career in front of this NBA player. I didn't want to reveal that I rode the bench at Florida State and average .7 points per game. But I had to tell him the truth even though it hurt.

The Justification Layer

Another layer is justification. We say things that we never really intend on doing like: "I'll pray for you." "I'll help you move." "I'll volunteer in the Children's Ministry." We say those things with no intention of doing them then justify the lie with thoughts like, "Well, I didn't want to hurt their feelings. I didn't want to step on their toes so I lied."

The Retaliation Layer

There's another layer—the retaliation layer. Let's say someone does something against us in the office. We just trump up a lie about them as quick as a tabloid reporter. We float it out there because we know that lie will hurt them. It's the retaliation layer, the retaliation lie.

The Confrontation Layer

Here's another layer. Many times we run from confrontation. We don't want to get into a confrontation with our spouse, boss, teacher or whoever so we just lie. We don't want the confrontation so we make up a lie to get out of it. "I didn't know you wanted me to do that." "I thought you were planning on taking care of that." Whatever it takes to get out of trouble.

The Exaggeration Layer

What about exaggeration? We say, "The fish I caught was this big." "I jumped ten feet high." "Oh my work schedule is ridiculously busy." Why do we do that? We lie by exaggerating and what does it really get us?

The Omission Layer

This is probably my favorite layer—the omission lie. Everything you tell is the truth, but you leave out critical parts of the truth. Let's say that you're a teenager and have a midnight curfew. You go to the game and get caught in traffic on the way home so you get home at 12:45. When your parents ask you why you are late you blame the traffic but leave out that you went to Sonic and hung out after the game.

Everything we say must be truthful, but we should not communicate all truth. People say, "She just tells it like it is" meaning they say everything they think. You're crazy if you do that. Imagine if I did that when I was conducting a funeral. I would be standing there with the guy's body right below me and say, "Hey, this guy was a nice guy but also he was a card carrying idiot because let me tell you what he did this one time...."

We've got to speak the truth. But that doesn't mean that we have to say everything that's on our minds. Some things are better left unsaid. So we've got to speak the truth but we've got to speak the truth in love.

3. Try to come up with some general principles for what things are true, but it is wiser to not say them.

_____

_____

_____

_____

A while back, I watched a young man grow up. He began telling lies to his parents and to his friends just to get out of stuff. No one ever confronted him and he never came clean. After he grew up, the truth whacked him and it was such a tragedy to see his marriage and family suffer the consequences. He was one prayer away from becoming a truth teller, but he never could step up and do it.

A lot of us are buried beneath layer after layer of lies and we don't even know it. There's the layer of guilt. There's a layer of disconnection between you and God. There's a layer of disconnection between you and others.

If you lie long enough your character corrodes. You lose any influence. You don't make an indelible impression on other people's lives because you are a liar. Life is

...TO LIE LIFE'S TOO SHORT

too short to live a lie. Come clean. Know the truth, Jesus said. It will set you free.

> *For the word of God is living and active. Sharper than any double-edged sword, it penetrates even to dividing soul and spirit, joints and marrow; it judges the thoughts and attitudes of the heart. Nothing in all creation is hidden from God's sight. Everything is uncovered and laid bare before the eyes of him to whom we must give account.* Hebrews 4:12-13

One day we are all going to stand face to face with the Lord and give an account of the words that we said. Did we tell the truth or did we lie? Were we honest or dishonest? Did we discover God's amazing agenda or did we do life with layers of lies and guilt that kept us from achieving the greatness that God desires?

The choice is up to you and me. It's been my prayer that we come clean and allow God's Word to penetrate and to peel back layer after layer of lies so we can discover who God wants us to become.

You may be asking, "Well, Ed, how do we do that? I've been living a lie. I've been doing the exaggeration thing, the omission thing and the elevation thing for so long. Is there hope for me?"

DO A WORD SEARCH

There is hope no matter how deep you are buried in lies. Here are a couple of suggestions for getting back to the truth. Number one, regularly do a word search when you pray.

We should pray everyday. And I challenge you to journal your prayers. When you journal your prayers take some time and say, "Okay God, let me run through the rolodex of my conversations. Today or yesterday, did I do the elevation thing? Did I justify something? Did I do the retaliation lie, the confrontation lie, the exaggeration lie or the omission lie?"

Stop and listen to God, because he will bring that stuff up. And when he brings that stuff up, it's time to come clean by confessing. The word "confession" means that we tell the truth about our condition. When we confess and say, "Hey, God, I've done this or I've done that," God is not going to say, "Oh, I didn't know that. Really? You've been lying? Thanks for letting me in…" No. God

LIFE'S TOO SHORT ...TO LIE

knows. He knows everything. He's everywhere. And, he's all powerful. So, there is no point in lying. Just confess.

Now the plot clots. This separates the tire kickers from the buyers. Christianity is not for people who need a crutch. It's not for quiche eaters. Scripture tells us that if we lied, we need to track the person down we've lied to, lock eyes with them and we've got to say, "I lied to you. Will you forgive me?"

4. What have you learned from confessing and asking for someone else's forgiveness?

_____

_____

_____

Ouch! It hurts when you have to say that. I've had to do that before when I've lied. All it takes is having to do it four or five times and you won't lie anymore! You'll think long and hard about telling that lie, about exaggerating, elongating or pontificating. You won't do it anymore.

INSTALL A LIE DETECTOR

Here's the second suggestion. After doing a word search, install a lie detector. Do you have someone in your life who loves you for who you are? Do you have someone in your life who will encourage you and who will pray for you? Do you have someone in your life who will hold you accountable for what comes out of your mouth, who will hold you accountable to truth telling? We need to.

5. If someone asked you to be their lie detector, what could you do to help them?

_____

_____

_____

_____

...TO LIE LIFE'S TOO SHORT

The church is all about one another. The Bible says we should serve one another, pray for one another, encourage one another and support one another. We should be accountable to one another. That's why we encourage people at Fellowship Church to get involved in a small group. If you are not in a small group and someone asks you to join, don't just say, "Yeah, I'll show up." Actually show up. Become a part of a small group and God will bring people into your life who will help you in this endeavor.

HIRE A GUIDE

Another suggestion is to hire a guide. Really, God's grace does this. The moment we become Christ-followers, Christ comes into our lives and he places the Holy Spirit in us. And the Holy Spirit works from the inside out to turn us into truth tellers. He prompts us to tell the truth. He convicts us when we are thinking about lying. And, he helps us come clean when we have lied.

> *But when he, the Spirit of truth, comes, he will guide you into all truth....* John 16:13

Do you remember the story about me having lunch with an NBA player, when I wanted to exaggerate? I felt the Holy Spirit saying, "Ed, what you are getting ready to do is going to be a lie." So I throttled back.

6. How have you recognized the Holy Spirit guiding you?

_____

_____

_____

_____

Every time we throttle back, we build character. Every time we throttle back and tell the truth, we make an indelible impression on other people's lives. Every time we throttle back, we become mature. Every time we throttle back, we become an awesome example for the world to see. Every time we throttle back, we discover God's powerful purpose for our lives.

LIFE'S TOO SHORT ...TO LIE

LIES WE BELIEVE

Life is too short to lie. It's also too short to believe a lie. I know that some of you are living a lie because you are believing the father of lies, Satan. And the lie you are believing is leading you to an eternal separation from God.

Some of you are believing the denominational lie. You think, "Hey, my father was a Baptist deacon. So, I guess that must mean I'm in." Or, "I grew up Catholic. I was an alter boy." Or, maybe you think that because you were baptized Lutheran or Episcopalian, or Church of Christ that you're in.

Those things aren't bad things, but denominations are man made. When you go to heaven, that label of Catholic, Baptist or whatever will blow off. But if you go to hell, it will burn off. If you are counting on your denomination to get you to heaven, it's not going to happen. A lot of you believe that lie. Some of you believe another lie.

You think, "I'm a good guy," or, "I'm a good girl. If I keep my nose clean, pay my taxes, throw a couple of bones God's way then I'm in. God must grade on this cosmic bell curve and you know, I'm better than most people. When I get to the end of my life, God will say, 'Hey, you were a lot better than you were bad, so come on into heaven.'" That's a lie. Based on what Scripture says, you're going to hell if you believe that.

7. What are other common lies that Satan tries to feed us?

_____

_____

_____

_____

TRANSFORMATIONAL TRUTHS

Those are lies we can believe that will create separation between us and God. But, we can resist those lies by believing some transformational truths.

God is Crazy About You

First of all, God is crazy about you. He loves you so much that you can't even comprehend it. He loves the world so much that he gave his only son who died on the cross for all of our sins. We don't deserve it. He just did it because he is crazy about you. And then he rose again. The Bible says if we receive that, if we open the door of our hearts and allow Jesus to infiltrate our lives, what happens?

An Exchange is Made

When we accept what Jesus did for us, the righteousness of Christ is transferred into our lives. All of our junk, our guilt, our sin and our mess ups are transferred onto the shoulders of Christ. So now, when God looks at me he sees Christ's righteousness instead of our sin. That's the only reason that I know I'm spending eternity with the Lord. It's not because of what I have done or haven't done. It's because of what Christ has done for me and that I've received that.

I want to give everyone an opportunity to make this decision. I made this decision years ago but I can't make it for you. This is between you and God. If you mean business with the Lord and want to tell the truth about your condition, just say these words "God, to the best of my understanding, I believe that you sent Jesus Christ to die on the cross for all of the junk in my life, all of my sin, all of my mistakes, all of my foul-ups, and all of my lies. And God, I turn from that and turn to you. I ask Jesus Christ to come into my life. I give him everything I am right now and everything I will ever be."

If you prayed that prayer with me, that's the most awesome thing you will ever do in your life and I want to congratulate you. I want to challenge you to tell someone about it. Tell someone in your small group or your church so they can celebrate with you and help you figure out what to do now.

WRAP IT UP

God has given us the precious gift of a life with him followed by an eternity in his unimpeded presence. There are so many other things we can fill our lives with, but we will miss out on what God has in store for us. The reality is that our time on earth is short so we need to maximize it by following God's plan.

8. If you had to add one more week to this study what would be the subject and why would you choose it? Life is too short to....

Notes:

Prayer Requests:

...TO LIE | LIFE'S TOO SHORT

STEP IT UP

Take a step further over the next few days and spend some time reflecting on the following devotional thoughts that reinforce the previous session. Use these as reminders to take what you've learned and apply it to your everyday life.

DAY 1

Can you name all of the Ten Commandments? You might not remember all 10, but here is an easy way to remember them. The first four commandments can be summed up as love God. The last six commandments can be summed up as love others. So if you want to sum up the 10 commandments you could say they teach us to love God and love others.

Read Exodus 20:16

Within the six commandments about loving others, we find a commandment about honesty. Part of loving others is being truthful. The difficult part is that sometimes the truth hurts. Is it right to share the truth even when it could hurt?

Honesty can be painful. It is not easy to tell a friend they are in a relationship that is unhealthy. Drawing boundaries with family is not a simple conversation. Being honest with ourselves about where we fall short is not fun. But, great growth and health can come from honesty.

God has called us to love each other, and that must be the foundation for honesty. There are many things we can say honestly, but without love. In those cases, the truth can be damaging. When we point out faults and criticize just to satisfy ourselves, that can be dangerous and damaging. We have to speak the truth out of love. And a love for others starts with our love for God. When we are in a love relationship with God, we will have a love for others.

Why do you think love is such an important prerequisite for honesty?

How could you make sure your honesty is built on the foundation of love?

LIFE'S TOO SHORT ...TO LIE

Notes:

Prayer Requests:

DAY 2

Deuteronomy 25:13-16

In the time this was written, if you wanted to buy something like grain, it would be weighed out on a scale. On one side of the scale, they would place the weights equaling the amount you wanted and on the other side of the scale they would place your product.

The problem with this system is the seller could shave down their weights. So, a weight that was supposed to weigh 1 pound might only weigh ¾ of a pound. The result is you would pay for 1 pound but only get ¾ of a pound.

God could not stand that dishonesty. It showed a lack of respect for others and a greedy selfishness. We don't need Old Testament weights to fall into the same trap. There are still dirty deals happening all around us.

If you are in a business where you give estimates, do you give a low estimate to entice a client then jack up the price once the work has begun? Do you pressure your friends to buy your products so you can meet your quotas? Do you hide key information in proposals to close the deal?

There are lots of ways we can deal dishonestly, and every one of them dishonors God. He desires honesty out of a love and respect for him and others.

Is there any part of your life where your dealings are questionable?

How could you go about your business in a way that honors God?

Notes:

Prayer Requests:

DAY 3

Psalm 139:1-4

Talk about reading your mail! God knows your life inside and out. The thought you are having right now as you think about God knowing the intimate details of your life—God knows it. There is nothing you can hide from God: not only your actions, but also your motivation. God knows what truly motivated you in each and every decision.

That can be a scary thought. If we see God as some angry principal waiting to punish us, we are in trouble. But what if God is not an angry principal? What if God is more like a loving doctor who wants to see you healed from a terminal illness? In that case, you would want God to know every intimate detail. You would want him to know your exact condition so he could heal you.

God knows that sin is a destroyer. It poses as the answer for what we want then turns into a disease that we cannot control. And God knows the potency of sin. He is so aware that he was willing to sacrifice his Son as a solution. Now he wants to enact that healing in all who are ready to be healed.

Do you want to experience God's healing touch? It takes honesty. We have to be honest before God with our sickness. We have to be open about our need for his healing. We have to accept when he shows us where our sickness has spread. Only in that complete honesty, can we find relief. In those moments of truth, we can find healing and wholeness.

Read Psalm 139:23-24, then make it your prayer to God.

LIFE'S TOO SHORT ...TO LIE

Notes:

Prayer Requests:

DAY 4

Luke 16:10-12

Can you be trusted? I think the first response for all of us is, "Of course I can be trusted!" And there are probably plenty of times you can be trusted. Most of us can be trusted in the major things. Most of us can be trusted when we promise we will come through this time. Most of us can be trusted when there are serious consequences for not coming through, but that is only part of being trustworthy.

Can you be trusted in the little things? That is where the rubber meets the road of trustworthiness. When you tell someone you will call them, do you? When you tell someone you will meet them at a certain time, do you show up 15… 30… 60 minutes late? When you get that bill in the mail, do you pay it on time or when you get around to it? Trust is proven in the little things.

We prove our trustworthiness to God and others in the little things. When God reveals something that needs to be tweaked in your life, do you address it? That could be an opportunity from God to show you are ready for something more. When a friend asks you to help them with something small, that could lead to opportunities to be more involved and influential in their life in the future.

Face it, the little things matter. So be trustworthy with the little things and you will be trustworthy with the major things.

How have you not been trustworthy this week?

What is a way you could become trustworthy in a little area this week?

Notes:

Prayer Requests:

DAY 5

Revelation 19:11

It is amazing what we can become known for. The girl who dropped her lunch tray in the third grade can carry that reputation all the way through high school. The high school jock can carry that reputation into his career. The career-driven executive can carry that reputation in her relationships. And the list goes on and on. We can become known for a multitude of things.

Jesus is the rider and he is known as "faithful and true." That is an incredible reputation. Jesus proved himself faithful as he lived a sinless life despite temptation. Jesus was faithful as he endured the cross for our sins. He has been faithful to all who called on his name for salvation.

Jesus is true. He proved it while he walked the earth as he demonstrated he truly was God. He demonstrates his truthfulness as his promises for life are fulfilled in the lives of believers. Jesus even went as far as to say he is the embodiment of truth (John 14:6).

Jesus is rightfully known as faithful and true. What are you known for? The decisions you make will determine your reputation. You are not known for what you would like to have done. You are not known for how you should have acted. So don't miss the opportunity to follow Jesus' lead and be known as faithful and true.

Based on the decisions you make now, what are you known for?

What is something you would like to be known for and what decisions could you make to earn that reputation?

Notes:

Prayer Requests:

LEADER'S GUIDE

...NOT TO FISH

LEADER'S NOTES

2. **Describe your first experience going fishing. What stands out the most about that experience and what part did you enjoy the most?**

   Tip: If someone is an avid fisherman, see if he or she can articulate what hooked them on fishing.

3. **If you were in Jesus' shoes today and needed to assemble 12 disciples, what types of people would you choose?**

   Would they want an inner circle of like-minded people or is diversity a priority? What qualities are important to them? Help your group to push past just sharing who they would want and get them to also dig into why they would want them.

4. **Why do you think so many Christ-followers don't share Jesus' passion for being a fisher of men?**

   The most common answers will probably revolve around feeling awkward, not being confident in their biblical knowledge, or simply lacking the time to reach out. What we have to remember, though, is that God made each of us capable of fishing for men, and that we must make it a priority in our lives.

5. **If you have been fishing for very long, you have stories of ones that got away. Share some of your stories of people you have fished for that did not accept Christ?**

   Help your group to see beyond the disappointment of

115

...NOT TO FISH LIFE'S TOO SHORT

losing fish. They followed God's command, they planted seeds, but beyond that, the results were up to God. No matter how many get away, some don't, and that makes it worth the time and effort.

6. How does this verse take the pressure off you when you go fishing?

When we realize that we simply cast the line and that God does the catching, our anxieties can go out the door because we are not responsible for the end result. We just have to do our part by being eager fishermen, and leave the rest up to God.

7. How have you partnered with your church to go fishing?

First, we must invite the people we rub shoulders with to attend services or events. Second, we should serve as volunteers so that when guests come, their experience is as comfortable and exhilarating as possible. And third, we should be diligent with our tithes so that the church can continue to reach out.

CREATIVE NOTES

ICEBREAKERS

Name Your Passion

What do you get passionate about? Share with the group.

BRIDGE — God wants us to be passionate about sharing Christ with others.

Guess That Lure

Divide into two groups. Put out five lures with specific names and have groups write down their guess for the names of the lures. Then, compare answers to see what group got the most right.

BRIDGE — God has called us to be a fisher of men.

HANDS-ON ACTIVITIES

Map Quest

Pass out maps of the area and have each person place stickers on every place they usually go in a week (soccer game, work, school, Starbucks, cleaners, restaurant, around the neighborhood, etc). Brainstorm ways to connect with the people you come in contact with to build relationships.

LIFE'S TOO SHORT ...NOT TO FISH

BRIDGE — We have the opportunity to influence a large area when we work together.

Casting Challenge

Get fishing rods and have a casting challenge to try to hit specific targets. Another idea is to use a child's fishing pole or fishing game to have a contest between members.

BRIDGE — God has given us a challenge to fish for men.

Prize Lure

Provide supplies such as pipe cleaners, feathers, ribbon, etc. for members to make a fishing lure. Have a prize for the winner.

BRIDGE — We should spend time in prayer over people God would have us try to lure to him.

VISUAL REINFORCEMENTS

Fishing Equipment

Rod, reel, net or fishing items in a tackle box.

BRIDGE — God has called us to be fishers of men.

TAKE HOME OBJECT

Goldfish

Give each a pack of goldfish crackers with Matthew 28:19-20 attached.

LEADER'S GUIDE
SESSION TWO

...TO BE NEGATIVE

LEADER'S NOTES

1. **Try to name all the magazines and television shows that are dedicated to airing celebrities' dirty laundry.**
   Tip: If you want to extend the icebreaker question, ask your group if they enjoy reading or watching celebrity gossip, and why or why not.

2. **How have you been burned by negativity; either by your own negative attitude or someone else's?**
   Hurt people, hurt people. So if we are around hurt people, their negative experiences can hurt us. They can turn their hurt on us and say things that are negative. Also, their negativity can become contagious. We can end up with a bad attitude that makes us miss out on the good around us and that can hurt those around us.

3. **How have you noticed that negative people bring out negativity in you?**
   If you are in a bad situation and someone starts complaining, it is tempting to join in. Their negative comments can lead us to focus on our negative thoughts and before we know it, we are just as negative.

4. **How have you experienced people grumbling against you when you tried to lead?**
   Leadership can be lonely, especially when followers don't understand your decisions. The thing to keep in mind, though, is that God expects us to execute his vision, not everyone else's. We have to be prayerful and steadfast leaders, not wavering people pleasers.

...TO BE NEGATIVE LIFE'S TOO SHORT

5. **What have you noticed in your life that causes you to go negative the most?**
   When something happens that we don't think is fair is a common time that we go negative. If we think we are not getting what we deserve or if someone else is getting something they don't deserve, negativity it tempting. Also, in stressful situations we can unleash negativity by letting down the filter between our brain and mouth.

6. **What are things you could do to find encouragement and hope without chasing down those who are negative?**
   Staying positive when you're surrounded by negativity takes two things; time with God and time with godly people. Pray, read the Bible, and talk to encouraging people who don't rain on your parade.

7. **Who are the replenishing people in your life and what makes them that type of person?**
   Tip: As your group shares who their encouragers are, ask them how much of their free time is spent with them. Sometimes the energy suckers in our lives can be close family members and longtime friends, and we spend too much of our time with them just because of their status. It's important that we have balance by spending plenty of time with people who replenish us.

8. **What could you do to help you see and communicate the positive around you?**
   As Christ followers, we have to train our brains to remember that God created the world around us. We have to praise him for the good things in life, and talk about his love and purpose in the midst of hardship. The ability to be overwhelmingly positive in all circumstances is one of the best ways we can show God's power to the world. It sets us apart and makes non-believers want what we have: unshakable peace and joy.

CREATIVE NOTES

ICEBREAKERS

TURN IT AROUND

Have members tell about situations that make them want to go negative (slow check out lines, kids arguing, running late, etc). Have the group discuss how each situation can be turned around to a positive.

LIFE'S TOO SHORT ...TO BE NEGATIVE

BRIDGE — God doesn't want us to go negative.

½ Empty or ½ Full?

Place a container filled half way with something. Have members vote on slips of paper whether the container is ½ full or ½ empty. Ask the group if they have any ideas why they see things as ½ full or ½ empty.

BRIDGE — Whether its natural for us to see the jar ½ full or ½ empty, God wants us to learn to be positive.

HANDS-ON ACTIVITIES

Jumper Cable Game

Bring a set of jumper cables to use in a positive/negative game. Ask a series of questions and have the players holding the positive end to come up with positive answers and the ones holding the negative end come up with negative responses (ex. someone cuts you off in traffic).

BRIDGE — God doesn't want us to go negative but to stay positive.

Positive/Negative Quiz

In the start it up section, the questions are posed: When you pulled into the church parking lot and were told where to park, what was your attitude? Pass out a short "Positive/Negative Quiz" not to be shared but just for personal introspection. Make up a few questions like:

When I pull into church and are told where to park, I tend to:

a. roll my eyes

b. complain out loud

c. try to get around the parkers to park where I want

d. wave at the parker and yell out the window, "You are doing a great job!"

BRIDGE — God may want to show you that you struggle with negativity or he may show you that you are doing a good job being positive.

Poster People

Make a poster with three columns labeled Drainers, Neutral and Replenishing. Have the group list characteristics of people in each group. Then have members think about what kind of friend they are and how they could work on being the replenishing type of friend.

...TO BE NEGATIVE | LIFE'S TOO SHORT

BRIDGE — Being a replenishing friend is intentional.

OxyClean It

Have a shirt with different stains on it. Use Oxyclean to see if it will remove the stains. You can have someone act it out like a commercial. You could also have multiple stained shirts and divide into teams and see who can get the stains out.

BRIDGE — Allow God to use this lesson to clean us.

VISUAL REINFORCEMENTS

Dirty Laundry

Hang dirty laundry on a clothesline in the room or leave in piled in a basket. You could also have a shirt with stains labeled slander, gossip, secrets, sarcasm, etc.

BRIDGE — God wants us to get past our dirty laundry and experience his cleaning.

Food Coloring

Drop food coloring into a pitcher of water to show negativity is infectious.

BRIDGE — Don't give in to temptation to be negative and work hard to not pass negativity on.

TAKE HOME OBJECTS

Battery

It's your choice to be positive or negative.

Travel Size Tide

Come clean before God.

Dirty Sock

Give each member a dirty sock to remind them to avoid negative thoughts.

OTHER

Changing Your Tune

Compile a list of the top five things that you complain about and commit to have a different attitude. You could also have a funeral for "I can't" and not allow it to be said again because it is dead.

LEADER'S GUIDE
SESSION THREE
...TO BE ENVIOUS

LEADER'S NOTES

1. **Describe a time you can remember being envious and what caused it?**

   What brought the envy out? Was it petty envy that is evident in middle and high school? Maybe the envy came out because someone has something you desperately want. Or, maybe the envy is arise from something you can't do or have.

2. **Do you view some sins as more acceptable than others? Read the list of sins in Galatians again and determine which ones are considered "acceptable."**

   Many people think "lighter" sins like envy or jealousy are normal and okay, but the reality is that they're not, and we shouldn't convince ourselves otherwise. God knows the pain and destruction we can experience when we get tangled up in seemingly acceptable sins, so he warns us against them.

3. **How have you seen insecurity related to envy?**

   There will always be people who look better, do things better, and have more stuff than we do. If we allow ourselves to envy them, we're headed for some major insecurity. We'll always feel bad about who we are and what we have because we're too wrapped up in everyone else. Instead, we need to find our security and contentment through our relationship with Christ and who we are in his eyes.

...TO BE ENVIOUS — LIFE'S TOO SHORT

4. How is the older brother's perspective flawed and how do we share his flawed perspective when we envy?

He's focused on what his brother has been given and what he hasn't. He's analyzing the scorecard and ignoring all of the blessings he's received. When we go green with envy, we do the same thing. We obsess over everyone else and ignore our own blessings. When we envy our friend's Mercedes Benz, we stop appreciating the Honda Accord that gets us from point A to point B every day.

5. How would you have felt if you were the first person hired? How would you have felt if you were the last person hired?

Most of us would feel cheated if we were the first person hired, and lucky if we were the last. Regardless of what order we started in, though, we should be grateful for the wages we were paid. If you're the first one at the office and the last one to leave, and your coworker makes more than you but barely works 40 hours, you have to learn to ignore his situation and simply be grateful for your job and your income.

6. How could you use Psalm 139 in a discussion with someone that is envious of another person's looks or abilities?

If you know someone who struggles with envy, it's good to remind them that they are exactly as God created them to be. Wishing they were like someone else is being unappreciative of God's workmanship. He has a plan for each of us, and we are who we are because of that perfect plan.

CREATIVE NOTES

ICEBREAKERS

First Thing

Name the first thing that comes to your mind when you hear the word "green".

BRIDGE — Now let's look at what it means to be green with envy.

The One Thing

What is the one thing you wanted as a child that you never got?

BRIDGE — As adults, God wants to teach us to focus on what he has given us.

LIFE'S TOO SHORT ...TO BE ENVIOUS

HANDS-ON ACTIVITIES

Envy Cheers

Come up with cheers that celebrate the failures of others. You could assign a male and female to act the cheers out like the Saturday Night Live cheerleaders.

BRIDGE — God doesn't want us to celebrate the failures of others and live a life of envy.

Sin Order

Have group rank the sins in Galatians 5:19-21 in order from the worst to the most acceptable.

BRIDGE — We like to rank sin but God sees sin the same.

Count Your Blessings

Pass out a note card for members to write down the top 10 blessings God has given them.

BRIDGE — When we start to see what we don't have, this will be a reminder of what we do have.

VISUAL REINFORCEMENTS

Pom Poms

Pom Poms remind us to have a "Yeah God!" mentality when someone else is blessed.

BRIDGE — God wants us to cheer the success of others.

MEDIA REINFORCEMENTS

"I'll Think of a Reason Later"

Play Lee Ann Womack's song "I'll Think of a Reason Later". It describes her envy of a woman she does not even know.

It's All Over TV

Play commercials designed to make us envious.

TAKE HOME OBJECT

Toothbrushes

Toothbrushes clean our fangs.

...TO BE ENVIOUS   LIFE'S TOO SHORT

OTHER

Going Green

Serve all green foods on green plates (salad, spinach, broccoli, etc). You could serve cupcakes with green icing that would turn everyone's mouth green.

LEADER'S GUIDE
SESSION FOUR

...TO BE SELFISH

LEADER'S NOTES

1. What's something you have unwisely held on to that has cost you?

There are times we hold on to an investment too long and end up losing money. It could be waiting too long to sell your house or trade in your car. There are also times we hold on to relationships too long. We should let them go but we cling to what could be instead of what it. There are also habits that are held on to that should be dropped as we get older.

2. Describe an area where you have built a track record with God that has produced confidence?

Tip: As members of your small group share their experiences, reflect how God rewarded their generosity with an abundance of blessings and confidence. Suggest that they write these experiences down so that when times are tough, they can go back and see what God has done for them in the past.

3. What are you the most tempted to be stingy with?

We're all stingy with certain things. For some it might be Godiva chocolates they secretly eat late at night while everyone in the house is asleep. For others it's their money. They hold on so tight to their wad of cash, they become known as "tight-wads." The problem with stinginess is the thing we treasure above everything

...TO BE SELFISH LIFE'S TOO SHORT

and everyone can end up damaging our relationships with others. Unless we turn our "thing-dom" over to God's kingdom, we end up trapped. Our possessions end up possessing us and can totally mess up the abundant lives God wants us to live.

4. **As heavy as the weight is trusting ourselves, why do you think so few people exchange that weight for trusting God to provide?**
Sin is all about trusting in ourselves rather than obeying God who knows what is best for us. In the Garden of Eden, Adam and Eve were given everything they could ever need or want. They enjoyed a daily face-to-face relationship with God. They were free to have everything in the garden but the fruit of the tree of knowledge of good and evil (for obvious reasons.)

Satan slithered into their lives and told them a bold-faced lie that surely they knew what was best despite what their creator had told them. "Besides, who needs God telling you what to do when you can eat this forbidden fruit and actually become like God?"

The evil one continues to tell us this same lie today: "Just make this shady but profitable business deal, do this illegal drug, have this extramarital affair, and then you'll be happy." Just as he did in the garden, Satan fails to tell us about the consequences of our actions; the FBI finds out about the shady deal, we get addicted to the drug, the mistress gets pregnant; eventually, we end up trapping ourselves and losing the abundant lives we were meant to live.

5. **What is something generous you could do this week?**
Get creative and challenge each other to "pay forward" the abundant life God has given you. Start by thinking about the God-given talents you can use to help others in your community and church during the next week. Brainstorm ways members of your small group can work together to serve someone who is less able or less fortunate. You don't have to spend a lot of money. The key is to use what you have to glorify God.

6. **How have you experienced God provide for you when you put his priorities first?**
It could be trusting God's principles for relationships and seeing a new health in that relationship. Or, there could be the moment you trust God with your finances and experience his provision. There are countless principles we can put as priority and experience God's provision.

LIFE'S TOO SHORT ...TO BE SELFISH

CREATIVE NOTES

ICEBREAKERS

Stinginess

Some of the most popular movie and television characters embody selfish characteristics. Make a list of fictional, stingy characters and ask the group to describe their actions and behaviors.

BRIDGE — We remember these fictional characters because of their selfish ways. How do you want to be remembered by the people in your life?

HANDS-ON ACTIVITIES

One and Ten

Hand each team member 10 nickels, pennies, $1 bills, marbles or pieces of candy then ask each person to return one to you. See how quickly they release the items.

BRIDGE — God freely gives us everything we need and asks that we only give him our first fruits or 10% of our income, in return. How freely do you give God your time, tithe, thoughts, etc.?

Plaster of Paris

Break the group into small teams and ask them to prepare Plaster of Paris mixture from flour, paste and water. Have a contest to see who can make the best mold of someone's hand.

BRIDGE — Open hands are much more visually appealing than closed fists. Our hands and hearts can become hardened when we don't stretch and share our God-given gifts with others.

VISUAL REINFORCEMENTS

Pick-up-Sticks

Place boxes of Pick-up-Sticks around the room.

BRIDGE — As selfish creatures we collect and gather as much as our appetites will allow. When we clutch Pick-up-Sticks our fists are closed. But in God's economy he graciously opens his hands and gives generously, just as he did with his Son, Jesus.

...TO BE SELFISH LIFE'S TOO SHORT

Sticky Business

On a poster board stick different colors of tape, a honey label, Velcro, chewing gum, a glob of glue, fly paper, etc.

BRIDGE — Sticky substances can create big messes and so can sticky, selfish human fingers and selfish intentions.

MEDIA REINFORCEMENTS

Movie: "Scrooge"

Play the first half of the movie when Ebenezer selfishly declines his employees' requests for time off during Christmas.

OTHER

Attitude of Gratitude

Identify a person in need in the community, homeless shelter, or a nursing home that could benefit from an hour of service from the small group.

Random Acts of Unselfish Kindness

Write various acts of kindness on note cards, place them in a hat and ask members to draw one and agree to complete the activity before the next small group meeting:

- *While in the drive-thru, pay for the dinner for the person behind you*
- *The next time you're at the dry cleaners, pay for someone's dry cleaning in advance for them*
- *Mow a neighbor's lawn and leave a scripture card on their door as encouragement*
- *Write a thank you note to* a firefighter, police officer or librarian

LEADER'S GUIDE
SESSION FIVE
...TO LIE

LEADER'S NOTES

2. **Why do you think we are so tempted to lie by elevating our past experiences or accomplishments?**

    Our self-esteem can be so tightly tied to our accomplishments we are tempted to exaggerate them. The most common question we ask each other at any social gathering is, "What do you do?" We don't want to look like a "nobody," so we make what we do sound more important than it really is by using words with multiple meanings. We all want to be thought of as important so it is tempting to elevate our experiences.

3. **Try to come up with some general principles for what things are true, but it is wiser to not say them.**

    This is a tricky and sticky situation. Unless it's something they can change, its usually not helpful to speak the truth to someone about their appearance, their mama's appearance, or their baby's appearance. Sure, if they have smudged their make-up, tell them about it and help them fix it, but if they can't fix it, let it go.

    The same is true about personality quirks or little idiosyncrasies. These oddities may grate on your nerves, but unless you have a suggestion for fixing it, don't go there. If speaking the truth will hurt someone and it's something that cannot be changed, just don't do it!

4. **What have you learned from confessing and asking for someone else's forgiveness?**

    Confessing and asking for forgiveness can be painful, but it can also be helpful. We can learn humility from

131

LIFE'S TOO SHORT ...TO LIE

having to ask for forgiveness. We can also learn to be more careful in our decisions so we do not have to go back and ask for forgiveness.

5. If someone asked you to be their lie detector, what could you do to help them?
You could call them out when they lie. Don't let them pass off something as the truth that isn't. Help them recognize what they are doing. Also, help them see the damage of their lies. Sometimes they may not be aware of what their lies are causing.

6. How have you recognized the Holy Spirit guiding you?
Recognizing the Spirit comes from experience. God might work through your conscious, a thought, a verse or another person. But when you sense the Holy Spirit guiding you, obey. When you obey, you build sensitivity to the Spirit but when you disobey, it builds callousness.

7. What are other common lies that Satan tries to feed us?
Satan has been lying to us since the Garden of Eden. His lies are designed to drive a wedge between us and God. He tells us, "You're a big-boy: You can do this on your own. You don't need God. You don't need the crutch of the local church. It doesn't matter if you tithe or serve. What's in it for you?" The Bible tells us Satan is the father of lies and gives us example after example of the consequences of believing his lies.

8. If you had to add one more week to this study what would be the subject and why would you choose it? Lie is too short to....
Discuss what they would like to add and what advice they would give that week.

CREATIVE NOTES

ICEBREAKERS

White Lie Game
Ask members to think of two things that are true about themselves and one thing that's false. As they go around the room and introduce themselves, tell each but don't tell which is true and which is false. (i.e. "I have two brothers and one sister—AND—I was an Olympic swimmer in 2003)

LIFE'S TOO SHORT ...TO LIE

BRIDGE — How well do you know your small group members? Could you recognize the true statements? Life's too short to live in falsehoods.

HANDS-ON ACTIVITIES

Tabloids

Pass around several different tabloid magazines that include sensational headlines and tall tales. Ask the group to identify as many probable statements in the articles in the midst of all the lies.

BRIDGE — When you live a life layered in lies, it becomes increasingly difficult to pinpoint the truth, but God can.

VISUAL REINFORCEMENTS

Dutch Dolls

Set ceramic Dutch dolls around the room (the large doll contains a smaller doll which contains an even smaller doll). Each doll represents a layer and something hidden.

BRIDGE — God wants us to pull back the layers and get to the truth.

Faux Pas

Ask a few volunteers to bring counterfeit or knock-off clothing or accessories like plastic rings, fake Louis Vuitton handbags, faux furs, hairpieces, play money, un-official sports memorabilia, etc.

BRIDGE — Sometimes it's difficult to detect the real from the fake. An object may look good on the outside but in reality it's counterfeit. Are we living as authentic Christians? Can our friends tell the difference?

Layered Food

Serve 7-layer dip, layered cake, or sushi rolls as a tasty visual reinforcement of the lesson.

BRIDGE — God wants us to peel back the layers and be honest.

MEDIA REINFORCEMENTS

Movie: "Liar Liar"

Play the portion of the movie where Mr. Reed (Jim Carrey) gets pulled over by the police for traffic violations or the section when Max Reed is on the playground

...TO LIE LIFE'S TOO SHORT

and tells his dad (Jim Carrey) about his birthday wish. Explain to the group how lies have consequences.

Song: "Voice of Truth" by Casting Crowns

Just before the Closing Prayer play "Voice of Truth" by Casting Crowns and ask members to reflect on Jesus' character and how he continually spoke and demonstrated authenticity to his disciples.

TAKE HOME OBJECT

Sometimes Things Aren't What They Seem

Give each member some play money, chocolate coins, a toy watch or a fake ring as a reminder of the falsity in our lives.

Outrageous, Contagious Joy

Five Big Questions to Help You Discover One Great Life

What if there was more to life than you ever thought possible? Something beyond your wildest dreams? What if your days and weeks consisted of more than just waiting for the next payday, or the next acquisition, or the next boyfriend/girlfriend, or the next fun fix, or the next happy feeling, or the next whatever? What if you could have a bigger, more meaningful life right now?

Ed Young shares five life-altering questions and eye-opening insights that will steer you to what he calls *Outrageous, Contagious Joy*. In this inspiring, straightforward guide, he shows you the way to improve your life and find your divine purpose. It all begins with five simple yet profound questions:

- *Does God want you to be happy?*
- *Where are you headed?*
- *Who are you running with?*
- *Why are you here?*
- *What are you working for?*

Created to help you think about where you are and where you are going, this remarkable book will give you very specific and practical steps that will revolutionize the way you think of —and carry out—your life, and lead you to *Outrageous, Contagious Joy.*

Buy your copy today!

Available on CreativePastors.com or anywhere good books are sold.

Berkley hardcover, 352 pages

CHECK OUT THESE OTHER STUDIES BY ED YOUNG AVAILABLE ON CREATIVEPASTORS.COM:

INEED2CHANGE.COM
Taking Steps Toward Making Change

Let's face it. We all have things about ourselves we want to change, whether they are big or small. And in this series, Ed Young teaches us that change—real change—comes only from God. And when we learn to partner and cooperate with him, we tap into the power that can radically change everything about our lives, forever.

COMFORTABLE
Expanding Our Comfort Zone

In this study, Ed Young teaches us the importance of stepping out of our comfort zone. And we see that the only way to experience the true comfort found in Jesus Christ is to make sure we get uncomfortable enough to do what he has called us to do.

JUICY FRUIT
A Study Of The Fruit Of The Spirit

In this in-depth study, you will discover what it means not only to produce spiritual fruit in your own life; you'll also learn how to reveal those characteristics to those around you. And you will discover how a life dedicated to these principles ultimately leads to the kind of satisfying, vibrant life that God has in store for each of us.

SEXUAL REVOLUTION
God Designed It. Culture Redefined It. Who Got It Right?

It's time to put the bed back in the church and the church back in the bed. In this study, Ed Young helps you get back to God's incredible design for sex, beginning with the important realization that God created this life-uniting gift.

A BOUT WITH DOUBT
Responding To Global Turmoil And Personal Doubt

Doubt is not a cosmic crime or a blockade to your spiritual growth. When we take our bouts with doubt to God, he will allow them to strengthen our faith and draw us closer to him. This study is designed to teach us the right response to doubt.

RETRO
Getting Back To The Basics

Juggling life's priorities can easily become complicated and complex. In this series, Ed Young takes a closer look at the essentials for a strong Christian life, including building the right friendships, involvement in the local church, developing biblical priorities and taking time to rest.

FORGIVENESS - THE REAL F-WORD
Unleashing The Power Of Forgiveness

Forgiveness feels great—as long as we are the beneficiaries. We like being forgiven, but it's not very fun when you have to ask for forgiveness. Through this study, we will discover God's powerful truths about this highly-charged subject of forgiveness.

SNAPSHOTS OF THE SAVIOR
Jesus—Up Close And Personal

So often when we think of Jesus' life, our photo album is limited and sketchy. In this powerful study of talks, Ed Young shares vivid images from the Bible to help provide a broader, panoramic view of Christ's mission and ministry.

THE CREATIVE MARRIAGE
The Art Of Keeping Your Love Alive

Disposable relationships and throw-away marriages permeate our culture. When the dream fades and the realities of life set in, many just throw in the towel. In this six-week study, Ed speaks openly and honestly about the hard work involved in a creative marriage and the lasting rewards of doing it God's way.

IN THE ZONE
How To Live In The Sweet Spot Of Success

Do you want to live a life in marked contrast to those around you? In this study, Ed Young shares powerful biblical principles about what it means to live a life blessed by God—to live *in the zone*.

THE TABLE
Casting The Vision For The Local Church

The foundational series for small groups by Ed Young uniquely relates different aspects of eating a special meal to our purpose as Christ followers. As we focus on serving others, it reminds us in a powerful way that there's always room at the table.

MISSION POSSIBLE
Everyday Leadership Principles For Everyday People

Leadership is influence and every one of us influences someone. Mission Possible examines the life of one of the great leaders, Nehemiah, as he accomplished a seemingly impossible task using timeless leadership principles. Improve your influence as you download the principles from the journal of Nehemiah.

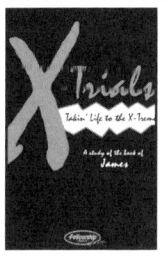

X-TRIALS – TAKIN' LIFE TO THE X-TREME
An Extreme Study In The Book Of James

In this book, X-Trials, Ed Young leads you through a verse-by-verse look at one of the most challenging and controversial books of the Bible, the book of James. Living life as a Christ follower in today's world requires extreme faith!

CHARACTER TOUR
A Biblical Tour Of Some Great Characters With Great Character

Certain character qualities stand out in notable characters throughout the Bible. In this creative series, Ed Young uses those great biblical role models to help us crack the character code and become people who live out godly character from the inside out.

VIRTUOUS REALITY
The Relationships Of David

People in your life can pull you up or drag you down. Join this journey into the life of David as we discover how this "man after God's own heart" lived out the daily reality of his relationships. By uncovering the good and bad in your relationships, Ed Young will help you discover how to honor God regardless of who crosses your path.

IGNITE
Refining And Purifying Your Faith

Fire, it is a source of destruction and a source of life. It incinerates and destroys. But it also refines and purifies. In the Bible, God used fire and other trials to turn up the heat and reveal His power through the lives of people. Ed Young explores these trials from Scripture to help fan the flames of our own faith today.

TRI-GOD
Understanding The Trinity

Three in One, One in Three. The Trinity. God in three persons—Father, Son, and Holy Spirit—is one of the most misunderstood doctrines in the Christian church. Yet, Ed Young teaches in this exciting new series that our awareness of God's triune nature is pivotal to growing with him.

FIRST AND 10
The Whats, Whys And Hows Of The Ten Commandments

Where do we find our moral foundation in this game of life? In a world of ever-changing culture, circumstances, and philosophies it all goes back to the big ten. Ed Young will take you on a thought-provoking, soul-searching look at the Ten Commandments.

WIRED FOR WORSHIP
Make Worship A Part Of Your Every Day Life

There is great debate and misconception surrounding "worship." One thing holds true, as human beings we are wired for worship. Whether it is career and finances or relationships and family, we instinctively worship something. Join Ed Young as he dives in to discover what it means to truly worship God in your life.

PRAYING FOR KEEPS
A Guide To Prayer

Imagine how awesome it would be to sit down and have a face-to-face conversation with God! In the small group study, you will learn how you can effectively and naturally communicate with God. Ed Young will walk you through the biblical principles that will guide you into a more intimate and rewarding life of prayer.

FATAL DISTRACTIONS
Avoid The Downward Spiral Of Sin

In this in-depth study, Pastor Ed Young makes a frontal assault on the seven deadly sins that threaten to destroy our lives.

RPMS - RECOGNIZING POTENTIAL MATES
Supercharge Your Dating Life

Whether you're a single adult, a student, or a parent, this creatively driven study will provide foundational principles on how to date and select a mate God's way. We're going to cruise past the cultural myths and embark on a supercharged ride to the ultimate relational destination.

MARRIAGE UNVEILED
Components Of A Healthy, Vibrant Marriage

This dynamic study uncovers the essential elements that will keep you growing together for a lifetime. Through this straight-forward, no-holds-barred approach, you will experience help and hope for troubled marriages as well as a challenge to make great marriages greater.